GENERAL PREFACE

THIS edition of Shakespeare aims primarily at presenting the text in such a way that it can be easily read and understood. The language of Shakespeare presents considerable difficulties to the beginner, difficulties which are soon forgotten and overlooked by readers who are familiar with the plays. The answers of examination candidates often reveal unexpected ignorance of quite ordinary Shakespearian phraseology and vocabulary. In the notes, therefore, the main emphasis has been placed on the interpretation of words and phrases. Textual and linguistic matter, to which much space was given in the old Clarendon Press editions of Wright and Clark, has been kept in the background, but explanation is prominent. The notes have been divided; words and phrases capable of a short explanation are glossed at the foot of the page, while the more difficult passages are treated after the text in the general commentary.

In the commentary alternative explanations and the mention of critics by name have been avoided as far as possible; on the other hand there are a number of less elementary notes on textual points and other matters not strictly necessary for younger students, and these appear in smaller type and within square brackets.

After the commentary is printed a substantial selection from the best criticism of the play, old and new; a feature in which this edition of Shakespeare follows the plan set by the Clarendon English series. Here some matter will be found suitable for more advanced students; and the inclusion of varying opinions will provide material for reflection and comparison. It is the editor's belief that students can best be taught to criticize by the provision of material which they may use as a starting-point as well as a model.

ACKNOWLEDGEMENTS

ACKNOWLEDGEMENT of permission to reprint copyright pieces of literary criticism is gratefully made to Messrs. Macmillan & Co., Ltd. (for Walter Pater, *Shakespeare's English Kings*, and for Sir Walter Raleigh's *Shakespeare*); to Mr. Stopford Brooke and Messrs. Constable & Co., Ltd. (for Rev. Stopford Brooke, *On Ten Plays of Shakespeare*); to Messrs. Kegan Paul, Trench, Trübner & Co., Ltd. (for E. Dowden, *Shakespeare: His Mind and Art*); to Messrs. Thornton Butterworth, Ltd. (for John Masefield, *William Shakespeare*); and to Messrs. William Heinemann, Ltd. (for George Brandes, *William Shakespeare*).

The text of Richard II *here printed is free from omission or alteration*

CONTENTS

THE FORTUNE THEATRE

A reconstruction by Mr. W. H. Godfrey from the builder's contract, which has survived. The theatre was built in 1600, two years later than the Globe, at which most of Shakespeare's plays were performed, and burnt down in 1621.

INTRODUCTION

DATE OF THE PLAY

The Tragedy of Richard the Second is related to the later History Plays in very much the same way that *Romeo and Juliet* is related to the later Tragedies. It has the same brilliance and conceits of language, the same immaturity in its characterization, and the same lyrical poignancy of feeling.

The latest date for the composition of the play is established by an entry for it in the Stationer's Register on August 29, 1597, for Andrew Wise, and by the publication of the first Quarto edition in that year. Most critics are agreed, however, that the play belongs to a somewhat earlier period of Shakespeare's workmanship, though there is little beyond purely internal evidence to support this opinion. There are marked resemblances in the play to Marlowe's tragedy of *Edward II* (1590–3); and some of Shakespeare's variations from Holinshed, notably with regard to the Queen, agree with those made in the second edition of Daniel's *Civil Wars* (1595). Most probably Daniel was the borrower and had seen the play performed; but of this we cannot be certain. Sir Edward Hoby invited Sir Robert Cecil to his house, on December 9, 1595, 'where... a gate for your supper shall be open and K. Richard present himself to your view'. We *surmise* that 'K. Richard' was a play, and that the play was Shakespeare's: but again this is guesswork.

This somewhat unsubstantial evidence for a date of composition earlier than 1597 has, however, strong support from the nature of the play itself. It shows a much closer adherence to his source than is usual with Shakespeare; not only does he follow the chronicle with unusual care, but he also introduces no elements of sub-plot or of humour, such as he employs in his maturer works. The presence of a large portion of rhyme is a mark of early work in Shakespeare, unless there be some special reason for it, such as when the play has a considerable element of Masque (e.g. *A Midsummer Night's Dream* and *The Tempest*); and one-fifth of *Richard the Second* is in rhyme. The blank verse is of the end-stopt variety, with relatively few 'double' and 'feminine' endings. The style is marked by numerous and elaborate conceits, puns, alliteration, antitheses, and general affectation of expression. The character-drawing, save in two or three of the leading persons, is immature; in few of his plays has Shakespeare presented so flat and undistinguished a group of minor people. All the internal tests, then, both those of verse-measurement and the more intangible tests of style and character-creation, indicate that the play is a comparatively early work. Yet neither the following of his source nor the imitation of Marlowe is so close as in his earliest history plays. It is therefore usual to place it somewhere in the years 1593–6.

POSITION AMONG SHAKESPEARE'S PLAYS

The Tragedy of King Richard the Second forms part of a trilogy, of which *Henry the Fourth* (Parts I and II) and *Henry the Fifth* are the other members, and it derives part of its wider significance from its place in that group. Broadly, the trilogy is concerned with the nature of kingship, with the question, for instance, of whether the inheritance of a crown justifies the exercise of kingly authority when the inheritor is obviously incompetent, and whether the possession of the ability and the opportunity to govern justifies the exercise of these to the extent of usurpation. *Richard the Second* forms a kind of lyrical prelude in the series, on the theme of poetic and self-willed ineptitude; *Henry the Fourth* presents a picture of harsh efficiency, the struggle and relative failure of an able usurper to win his subjects' hearts; whilst *Henry the Fifth* shows us the man at once born to be king and fit to occupy the office. He has the imagination and rough *camaraderie* which his father lacked, and which win for the son popular forgiveness of such faults as he has; he has also the strong sense of justice and native energy lacking in Richard, which enable him to manage the nation's business at home and abroad. The 'Henry' plays in the series have a large element of boisterous comedy and a richness of characterization which make them almost different in kind from *Richard the Second*, to describe which one must resort to metaphors from music, and it is this distinction which makes it difficult to believe that Shakespeare projected the series from the beginning as a whole. On the other hand the poet casts a prophetic eye to the future so frequently in the play that one cannot but feel he is already thinking of *1 Henry IV*. There are emphatic references to Bolingbroke's unquiet reign both by Richard and Carlisle (III. iii. 95 ff.; IV. i. 134 ff.); the gist of the serious action of *1 Henry IV* is given in a dozen lines spoken by the deposed king to Northumberland (V. i. 55–68); already Percy is presented as younger than he really was, and is associated with that Prince Hal the contrast of whose character and activities with his own was to occupy so large a part of the succeeding play (V. iii. 13 ff.); Prince Hal is already a source of anxiety to his father, as he continued to be; and finally, *Richard II* ends, and *1 Henry IV* opens, with the usurper contemplating a penitential voyage to the Holy Land.

THE TYPE OF PLAY

Strongly linked as the play is thus seen to be to the others in the series, it differs markedly from them in nearly every way. In *1* and *2 Henry IV* and *Henry V* Shakespeare made his greatest contribution to the 'Chronicle' or 'History' type of play by relieving and enlivening the ceremonial pageantry of history with a vigorous and substantial comic element in prose. But *Richard II* is without prose, and almost without humour, and approximates, both in title and in fact, much more nearly to tragedy than to comedy. It belongs essentially to the type of tragical history which Marlowe had created in *Edward the Second.* That dramatist, scornfully dissatisfied with the earlier type of chronicle play, which was frequently a mere dramatized version of events loosely connected by falling within one reign, or happening to one person, endeavoured to create in *Edward II* a type of drama which should be an organized unity through its interpretation of character and its relating of character to events. What a man was should show itself in what happened to him and in what he made to happen. With this new conception of its possibilities in its creators' minds, the 'history' play ceased to be a loose-jointed thing of rambling inconsequence and achieved something of the design and the unified impression of a higher work of art. It is this which gives their power to *Richard II* and *Richard III*, and whilst in the latter Shakespeare is much more strongly influenced by Marlowe, in both he is merely carrying to further perfection of development the type of chronicle-history which Marlowe had created.

STRUCTURE OF THE PLAY

Although he achieved, then, in *Richard II*, a unity of design and of atmosphere unusual in the history play, Shakespeare was not able to throw off altogether the inheritance of undramatic chronicle. In some of the Introductory Notes to the various scenes in this edition it is pointed out that what Shakespeare does is to take the audience rapidly over a series of events by means of a sequence of 'entrances'. Sometimes these 'entrances with announcements' are arranged so as to form a climax, as in Act III, scene ii; more frequently one feels that the dramatist has not thought of the scene as moving to a crisis within itself, but has used it as a means of bridging the time between events and of communicating information—for instance, in Act II, scenes ii and iii. This does not prevent the play from being what Sir Edmund Chambers calls it, 'a marvel of workmanship'; 'situations and phrases', he goes on to say, 'constantly recur in the second half of the play which are pointed inversions of others at the beginning.' The actual events lent themselves to this reversal of situation, with all its consequent irony; 'the history forms the plot'; Richard himself uses the pointed analogy of the two buckets. It is to Shakespeare's credit that he does not obscure the Nemesis-action with any intervention of sub-plot; the grim outlines of the events as they occurred are allowed to impose themselves on our imaginations with undiminished dramatic impressiveness. We see the banishment of Mowbray and Bolingbroke as part of a course of injustice upon which the King has entered; we see him pursue that path, reckless of what may follow, in spite of Gaunt's and York's warnings and protests; we see vengeance follow in Bolingbroke's justified return, and the consequent submission and deposition of the King. Then follows, as though some celestial dramatist were at work, the inevitable reaction and period of suspense in Aumerle's conspiracy, well calculated to fill the always-difficult interval between the crisis of the action and the dénouement. That conspiracy is admirably adapted to make Richard's murder a less unreasonable butchery, for it is obvious from it that while Richard is alive there can be no peace for the usurper. The arrival of Richard's body in London is as 'music at the close' of these events. It is no wonder that the 'lamentable tale' of this king caught the popular imagination long before it came to be rendered in drama, and that all that the dramatist had to do with it was to give it the 'other harmony' of verse. That he did more, that he made the story more humanly personal, founded the whole securely on character and passion, heightened the effects, and made beautiful what had before been merely painful, no reader of Holinshed or of history will deny; but the gods were good to him when they presented him with such a story ready-made.

CHARACTER OF RICHARD

Apart from the poetry, the main interest of the play is in the character of Richard. It is commonly said that we occupy ourselves with the clash of wills between the King and the usurper. There is no such clash. Though they may appear on the same scene, the steam-roller and the butterfly do not contend with one another; and yet the latter is not altogether discredited! When Bolingbroke refuses to make peace, it is the King who does what his subject wishes and proclaims a Trial by Combat; when Bolingbroke returns, Richard without persuasion begins to speak as a deposed monarch. The King is protected by a position which gives him power to inflict death, by a tradition of divine right widely accepted (and strongly emphasized by the dramatist), and by the loyalty of many subjects; hence his rival must move warily; but there is no struggle. Observe that even after Bolingbroke is on the throne, our interest is concentrated largely upon his victim—on his parting from his Queen, on his thoughts in prison, on the desperate courage of his end and the pathos of it. It is not the business of this Introduction to detail the features of the various characters; the student will build up for himself studies of the *dramatis personae*; but too much time can hardly be given to the interpretation of the subtle moods and changes, the soaring flights and the dying falls, of the King himself. His is not a character to satisfy the dramatist by moving steadily to action with consistency of will; it is rather acted upon, than acting; and its capricious and obstinate selfishness and cruelty when it does act make the spectacle at times a painful one. But to the student of human nature its brilliant glitterings are a sort of illumination in themselves; and they provide incomparable opportunities for verse.

THE MINOR CHARACTERS

The minor characters fall short of the richness of Shakespeare's later plays. Gaunt is admirable, in many ways; but he is rather an eloquent symbol than a man; and the dramatist could not afford to give very much attention to one who was to pass so early out of the play. York is a puzzle, and would almost deserve the description given to him by Swinburne—'an incomparable, an incredible, an unintelligible, and a monstrous nullity'—were it not that his inconsistent actions make him almost equally a puzzle in the chronicles themselves. The Queen exists to display Richard. Mowbray has a reserve of quiet power which reveals itself more in his exile than in what he does in the play. And the 'caterpillars of the commonwealth', as is perhaps fitting, we could not tell apart.

BOLINGBROKE

Only in Bolingbroke, who is not a 'minor' character, do we sense a personage of major proportions, and for various reasons he is not exhibited in full. His motives are often obscure to us, for we do not see him 'from the inside'; if we did, we should probably find him making self-justifying excuses for himself, as Richard does, for he has to do some things which need excusing and for which no excuse is possible; perhaps his silence is better. He has to profess a loyalty he does not feel or mean; he has to make vows, as that regarding the purpose of his return, which he allows himself to break; he has to 'suggest' Richard's death, and to discredit the friend who brings it to pass; however we may try to blind ourselves to the truth, he is a liar and a murderer. The great characters of Shakespeare, the Hamlets, the Othellos, are not of this kind; or if they be, like Macbeth, they have some redeeming quality of imagination; and the end of the play does not find them triumphant.

TRAGIC IMPRESSION OF THE PLAY

This circumstance alone would be enough to rob the drama of the highest tragic effect. We cannot feel fully sympathetic towards Bolingbroke and yet he has to be left in possession of the stage. It detracts from the power of the play, also, that Richard's fate was somewhat too well deserved for us to feel for him the full measure of tragic pity. Greater crimes than he commits we could forgive, were they accompanied with greater virtues; only, it is not through an excess of strength that Richard sins, but through irritating weakness. He can lavish on himself all the sympathy that the situation calls for; but when he has to think of others, such as Gaunt or his subjects, his imagination becomes morally blind. He is not of the stuff of which great tragic heroes or great tragic criminals are made.

And yet, in spite of these shortcomings inherent in the circumstances and the characters, the play is a deeply moving one. Its effect is mainly one of intense pathos. We witness as it were the destruction of a beautiful thing by something more coarsely adapted to life's uses, to the accompaniment of much lyrical verse. Not that the poetry of the play is all in the vein of lyrical pathos. When

Bolingbroke is enraged, his words take on the denunciatory power of a Hebrew prophet:

> Which blood, like sacrificing Abel's, cries
> Even from the tongueless caverns of the earth,
> To me for justice and for chastisement.

It is not only on his death-bed that Gaunt is eloquent. Such lines as

> Thou canst help time to furrow me with age,
> But stop no wrinkle in his pilgrimage,

or

> All places that the eye of heaven visits
> Are to a wise man ports and happy havens,

have power to move scarcely less than his famous 'England' speech. Mowbray's lesson on reputation to his sovereign is hardly less eloquent. Or, as in the Combat scenes, Shakespeare can give his verse the force and brazen quality of a trumpet. How vividly contemptuous he can be at will is well seen in Richard's

> Off goes his bonnet to an oyster-wench;
> A brace of draymen bid God speed him well,
> And had the tribute of his supple knee.

Or take such thumb-nail sketches, of a line each, as deserted Plashy, with its 'Unpeopled offices, untrodden stones', or Gloucestershire, with its 'High wild hills and rough uneven ways', or Langley garden, with its 'dangling apricocks'. One is apt to forget such beautifying touches as these in the larger eloquence of Gaunt's and Richard's expressions of their love of England, or of Carlisle's and the King's prophetic denunciations, passages which have made the play famous. Yet it is, we feel, these rarer beauties which make one return to it and which place it higher in the estimate of literary critics than its public reputation has perhaps warranted. The more full-voiced passages we learn by rote may sometimes pall; but not the tenderness without weakness of

> Good sometime queen, prepare thee hence for France,

or the noble dignity of

> I am sworn brother, sweet,
> To grim Necessity, and he and I
> Will keep a league till death.

SOURCE AND TREATMENT

Shakespeare drew practically all his material for this play from Raphael Holinshed's *Chronicles of England, Scotland, and Ireland*, first published in 1577. Probably he used the second edition, of 1587, since the portent of the withering of the bay-trees (II. iv. 8) is not recorded in the first.

For some minor points Shakespeare appears to have been indebted to writers other than Holinshed. The latter, for instance, says that Carlisle on his arrest was handed over to the Abbot of St. Albans. Shakespeare correctly gives him to the Abbot of Westminster. In this detail, as in the statement that York is old (V. ii. 114), the dramatist is probably following Edward Hall's *Union of the Noble and Illustre Famelies of Lancastre and York* (1542). To Stow's *Annals* he probably owes the mention of Norfolk's journey to the Holy Land (IV. i. 92–5), of which Holinshed says nothing. Lord Berner's translation of Froissart may have supplied the account of Richard's public renunciation of the crown, which conflicts with what Holinshed has to say. Daniel, in the second edition of his long poem, *The Civile Wars between the two houses of Lancaster and Yorke* (1595), agrees with Shakespeare in making the Queen not a girl but a woman, in describing an interview between her and the King *after* his return to London, and in having Richard and his captor ride into London together; but which author was the borrower is impossible to tell with certainty. We suspect that it was Daniel.

What Shakespeare may have owed to other plays on the same theme is again impossible to estimate. Dr. Simon Forman records in his Diary for April 30, 1611, that he saw a play of *Richard II* at the Globe Theatre. It included the Wat Tyler rebellion and ended before the deposition. It is not now extant. There is in the British Museum a manuscript play of *Richard II*, which scholars assign to the years 1590–5. It deals with an earlier part of the reign than does Shakespeare's play, but it is thought that Shakespeare probably knew it. On the other hand, there seems no doubt of his having known and in some ways imitated Marlowe's *Edward II*, particularly in the abdication scene, and emulation of that author was probably a stronger stimulus than the seeing or reading of the play above mentioned.

In an appendix will be found extracts from Holinshed's Chronicle; the student should study them in relation to the play and make a list of the changes Shakespeare effects, with suggestions as to why they were made: nothing will so clearly bring home to him what the dramatist was about. It should be kept in mind that the business of the chronicle is to record what happened, whether it makes a pointed story or a dramatic incident or not, whereas the drama has to present an action with a beginning, a middle, and an end, that is, a unity of events closely-woven in cause and effect. It is under this law that Shakespeare effects most of his changes. He makes the Queen a grown woman, instead of a girl of twelve, because her presence as a woman enables him to reveal much in Richard's character, whereas if she had her real age she would merely be in the way. The poet makes the Duchess of York of the play Aumerle's mother, which she was not, but his change supplies him with a contrast to York and a source of much convincing activity throughout two scenes. So with Gaunt, who from the unscrupulous and self-seeking politician, the unsuccessful general, and the unpopular administrator known to history, becomes the embodiment of patriotism. He is necessary to Shakespeare as a symbol, as a contrast to Richard's selfishness, as the voice of the absent Bolingbroke, and indeed of England; and so he is exhibited as we find him. In the same way the poet disregards time and distance, so that Bolingbroke is only leaving England when it is reported that he has already been to France, has had his marriage to the French king's cousin prevented by Richard, and has now landed at Ravenspurgh to claim estates which Richard has just vowed to confiscate! The death of the Duchess of Gloucester is very effectively antedated to produce a cumulative effect. Aumerle, speedy traitor as he was, is not allowed time to abandon Richard's cause for Bolingbroke's, and then to conspire against his new patron, as actually occurred; he is made loyal to Richard throughout, since Shakespeare needs his plot against the usurping king to fill the stage immediately after the deposition.

It is clear that Shakespeare is creating a play which will be a unified story of circumstance and character, and not a mere dramatized version of a disjointed record of events, such as many chronicle plays then were. In this particular case the events, dependent as they were to so great a degree upon the character of Richard and Bolingbroke, certainly lent themselves to dramatic presentation; the dramatic contrast of character was already there in the story, and the dramatist admirably seizes on the events which led to Bolingbroke's banishment as the starting-point of the action which ended in Richard's downfall. For from that banishment there followed the chance offered to Richard to seize the estates, his consequent ability with the help of the money to absent himself in Ireland, Bolingbroke's exceedingly good excuse for returning, and the excellent opportunity presented to him of establishing his power in the King's absence.

The material offered by Holinshed was thus first-rate of its kind; yet it will be found that nearly all that gives its human quality to the drama is of Shakespeare's invention. The scene between Gaunt and the widowed Duchess; Gaunt's own death-bed; the pathetic incident at Langley, in York's garden; the moving scene of Richard's abdication; the parting of the deposed monarch and his Queen; the story of the groom, and the sorrowing of Bolingbroke over his dead rival—these are of Shakespeare's own making. In many of the scenes the action consists largely of a series of entrances with announcements; but in the scenes of Shakespeare's invention there is more consistency of feeling, less mere covering of ground; the turbulent feelings aroused by the action settle in a definite channel and rise to steady power; they strike some one key, and keep to it throughout; it is from them that we get a unified impression of the play, and the best of its poetry. So true it is that the best even of Holinshed's kind are but shadows, 'unless imagination amend them'.

SUMMARY OF RICHARD II'S REIGN

1377 Richard, aged 11, succeeds his grandfather, Edward III. John of Gaunt takes the lead in government.

1381 Wat Tyler's Rebellion, caused largely by Gaunt's oppressive taxation, put down by Richard.

1382 Richard married Anne of Bohemia.

1386 A Commission of eleven lords appointed to govern.

1387 The Commission declared to be illegal. Gloucester, Arundel, Warwick, Derby (i.e. Bolingbroke), and Mowbray, as Lords Appellant, impeach of treason five of Richard's ministers, and defeat his troops at Radcot Bridge.

1388 The Wonderful or Merciless Parliament condemns the king's friends to execution, imprisonment, or exile.

1389 Richard suddenly assumes reins of government.

1394 Death of Queen Anne.

1396 Richard marries Isabella of France, a child of eight, for political reasons; truce declared with France for thirty years.

1397 Richard has his revenge on the Lords Appellant. Gloucester is captured and put to death, Arundel executed, Warwick banished. Bolingbroke and Mowbray declare themselves his friends.

1398 Parliament meets at Shrewsbury. Bolingbroke accuses Mowbray. When they meet at Coventry both are banished.

1399 Richard raises money by forced loans, fines, and the confiscation of Lancaster's estates. Expedition to Ireland.
July, Bolingbroke lands at Ravenspur. August, Richard surrenders. September, Richard abdicates.

TEXT OF THE PLAY

Judged by the number of contemporary editions, *Richard the Second* was one of Shakespeare's most popular plays. Quarto editions appeared in 1597, 1598 (twice), 1608, 1615, and 1634; and the play was included in the Folio of 1623. It was thus 'the first genuine play by Shakespeare to obtain the honour of print after having been duly entered in the Stationer's Register', and the only one of Shakespeare's plays to appear in three editions within two years. As we shall see presently, there were particular reasons for this popularity, apart from the merits of the play.

It was the custom of Elizabethan times to use the title-pages of books as a sort of advertisement; accordingly that of the first Quarto of this play reads: 'The / Tragedie of King Ri/chard the se-/cond. / *As it hath been publikely acted / by the right Honourable / the Lorde Chamberlaine his Ser-/vants.* / LONDON / Printed by Valentine Simmes for Andrew Wise, and / are to be sold at his shop in Paules church yard at / the signe of the Angel. / 1597.'

The publisher, it is to be noted, does not trouble about the author's name; the two editions of 1598, however, are stated to be 'By William Shake-speare'. Some high authorities explain the omission of the author's name in the first Quarto by saying that even in 1597 Shakespeare's reputation could not have been very great. It is hard to see how it could have become so great by the following year as Francis Meres's mention in his *Palladis Tamia* (1598) clearly shows it to have been, if in 1597 a bookseller did not think it worth while to put Shakespeare's name to a book. There is very probably some more satisfactory explanation.

In 1603 the book was assigned by Andrew Wise to Matthew Lawe, who in 1608 brought out a new edition, one issue of which has the title as before, whilst the other has a different title-page: 'With new additions of the Parlia/ment Sceane, and the deposing / of King Richard, / As it hath been lately acted by the Kinges / Majesties servants, at the Globe /'. Both issues have the scene of Richard's abdication (IV. i. 154–318), which is not given in previous editions. These lines, 165 in all, were printed in all subsequent editions of the play.

The Folio was apparently printed from the Quarto of 1615, but with many corrections; it gives the best text of the new lines, though it omits some fifty other lines from various parts of the play. For all but the added lines, the first Quarto gives the best text. The division into Acts and Scenes is first made in the Folio (1623).

This edition follows the text of the *Oxford Shakespeare*, except in I. iii. 20; II. i. 240; III. iii. 52 and IV. i. 210.

THE SIGNIFICANCE OF THE 'NEW ADDITIONS'
IV. i. 154–318

The deposing of a king was a dangerous theme for an English dramatist in the later years of Queen Elizabeth's reign. In 1570 the Pope had issued a Bull of Excommunication and Deposition against Elizabeth; he had sent his benediction to the Armada in 1587; and in 1596 he issued a second Bull inciting Elizabeth's subjects to rebellion. Elizabeth felt the weight of criticism directed against her. To William Lambard, the Keeper of the Records of the Tower, she said, on being shown the items under Richard the Second's reign, 'I am Richard the Second; know ye not that?' (Raleigh and Robert Cecil, too, it would appear, used the term 'Richard the Second' with some political significance now obscure.) Sir John Hayward, an historian, was arrested and imprisoned (1599–1600) because he had described the fall and deposition of Richard, and had assigned reasons for them, in his 'First Part of the Life and Raigne of Henrie IIII, extending to the end of the first yeare of his raigne' (1599). The Queen persuaded Bacon to find seditious utterances in it; she even suspected (since the author was a partisan of Essex) that the real author was shielding himself behind Hayward's name.

On the afternoon of the day before the attempt made by Essex to raise a rebellion in London (February 7, 1601), some of his friends and fellow conspirators persuaded the actors of Shakespeare's company, against their will, to perform 'the play of the deposing of King Richard the Second'; when the actors protested that the play was old and would not draw an audience, they were paid forty shillings to insure them against loss. Apparently it was anticipated that the spectacle of the abdication of Richard would favourably predispose the minds of the people to a similar act on Elizabeth's part. It is by no means certain that the play performed was Shakespeare's; we know that there were other plays on the same theme; but the odds are in favour of Shakespeare's company acting Shakespeare's play on this occasion. In any case, it is clear that a play such as this might be held—and in fact *was* held—to have significance relative to contemporary events. It was probably with this in mind that some responsible person omitted the 165 lines from all editions prior to Elizabeth's death; he desired to keep his head on his shoulders. Political circumstances were probably also responsible for the unusual number of editions of the play within a few years.

The omitted scene seems to have been part of the play as originally composed. It is difficult to imagine a dramatically satisfactory performance without it, even though a genuine crisis of the action comes in an earlier scene. In style it harmonizes with the rest of the play. And, most convincing evidence, it is hard to believe that the Abbot's words (IV. i. 321) 'A woeful pageant have we here beheld' do not refer to the scene of abdication which immediately precedes them.

THE PLOT OF THE PLAY

The action of this play might be described as a Nemesis one, in that it exhibits the doing of an unjust deed and follows the consequences as they return upon the head of the doer. Scenes i and iii of Act I show Richard incapable of governing his unruly nobles, and settling their quarrels in a way that is unsatisfactory to them and fraught with danger to himself. Scenes ii and iv of Act I emphasize his guilt, his dependence on favourites, his suspicion of Bolingbroke, and his callousness. In scene i of Act II Richard, already shown to be guilty of Gloucester's murder and of misrule, takes, by his seizure of Gaunt's estates, exactly the step that most surely leads to his destruction, for by this act he (1) alienates his nobles, whose fear of similar treatment for themselves is now greater than their jealousy of Bolingbroke's ambition; (2) gives Bolingbroke a good excuse to return from banishment with apparent justice on his side; (3) solves the problem of supplies for the Irish expedition—and so is enabled to be absent when he is most needed at home!

Thereafter the action shows the gradual closing-in of the inevitable consequences upon Richard—the landing of Bolingbroke and the steady growth of his power, the late return of Richard to an alienated kingdom and a disbanded army, and the final cession of the crown. The speeches of the Queen in Langley Garden, and later of the King, at the abdication, and, finally, of both together in their parting, are as it were pathetic lyric accompaniments to the latter part of the action; those of Bolingbroke to the condemned parasites, of the gardeners, and of York (in his account of how Bolingbroke entered London) sound a different note!

The new king is shown settling with patience and firmness the quarrels of his nobles, forgiving an enemy and making a friend, and by his quick determination doing his utmost to prevent civil broil. But the presence of the deposed monarch in the country is a continual danger; he has friends who are loyal and persistent; it was inevitable that Bolingbroke should wish him out of the way. Richard's death is prepared for by a kind of lyrical prelude in the scene with the groom and is surrounded with pathos. Bolingbroke's reception of Exton is a jarring note at the end; it probably satisfied Elizabethan sentiment regarding regicides; but a less unjust reproof and a greater expression of deep personal guilt would be more satisfying to modern feeling.

The following is an indication of the course of the action scene by scene:

I. i. At London Richard hears from their own lips the details of the quarrel between the Dukes of Hereford and Norfolk. He endeavours to compel a reconciliation between them, fails to do so, and allows that the quarrel be settled in a Trial by Combat to be held at Coventry.

I. ii. The Duchess of Gloucester in vain seeks redress at her brother-in-law Gaunt's hands for the wrongful death of her husband. The King's guilt in the matter is apparent; but Gaunt argues that since the King is God's substitute, the quarrel is God's. The Duchess directs our minds forward by her hopes for Bolingbroke's success in the tournament.

I. iii. The elaborate preparations are carried out for the Trial by Combat—the repetition of charges, farewells of the combatants to the King, &c.—to no purpose: Richard stops the proceedings at the last moment, deliberates with his council for a little, then pronounces sentence of banishment for ten years on Bolingbroke, for life on Mowbray. Later, he remits four years of Bolingbroke's sentence.

I. iv. Aumerle gives an account of Bolingbroke's departure: the King reveals that he suspects Bolingbroke's intentions. He proposes to depart for Ireland when news is brought (welcome to him!) that Gaunt is dying and requests his presence.

II. i. Gaunt delivers himself, first to his brother the Duke of York and later to the King, of a tirade against misgovernment and of a pæan of patriotism. Gaunt is removed and news comes of his death. The King proposes to seize Gaunt's goods: York protests—in vain. When Richard departs, the Lords complain of his conduct and propose to help Bolingbroke, who is on his way to England.

II. ii. The Queen's mood of foreboding is found to be justified when Green brings news of Bolingbroke's landing and of the support he is winning. York comes to announce his helplessness. A report arrives of the Duchess of Gloucester's death. York bids the nobles muster at Berkeley. The caterpillars of the State, Bushy, Bagot, and Green, disperse to Bristol or Ireland.

II. iii. Bolingbroke wins the support of Northumberland, Percy, Ross, Willoughby, in turn, and counters York's protests with the assertion that he has only come to claim his own: York has to let things take their course. Nevertheless Bolingbroke proposes to follow the 'caterpillars' to Bristol Castle, to punish them there.

II. iv. The King's troops in Wales disperse, since he fails to appear; the air is full of rumours regarding him.

III. i. Bolingbroke at Bristol sends the parasites to execution. He proposes to proceed against Glendower and others.

III. ii. Richard lands in Wales and greets his kingdom with elaborate expressions of affection. But Salisbury recounts the disbanding of his troops, Scroop the flocking of the nobles to Bolingbroke's support, and York's inability to stay the progress of the usurper. In despair, Richard goes to Flint Castle.

III. iii. Bolingbroke sends to Richard, in Flint, an affirmation of his allegiance and readiness to lay down arms provided he gets back his lands. After some delay the King sends a favourable reply; he and Bolingbroke meet, and he is virtually made prisoner by his rival.

III. iv. The Queen's ladies try to comfort her in the garden at Langley, while the gardeners express the popular opinion of the King's misrule. The deposition of the King is imminent.

IV. i. After Bagot has given evidence regarding Aumerle's

complicity in Gloucester's murder and his opposition to Bolingbroke's return, squabbling breaks out among the nobles and a series of challenges follows. Mowbray's name is introduced into the quarrel and Bolingbroke proposes to recall him, but the Bishop of Carlisle reveals that he has died in exile.

York comes to announce the abdication of Richard. Carlisle protests against it and prophesies disastrous consequences. Bolingbroke sends for Richard to make a public declaration of his abdication. Richard finally gives the crown to Bolingbroke. Northumberland insists that the abdicated king read a list of his crimes against the state. Richard in despair asks that a mirror be brought, so that he may see the change wrought in his face by his misfortunes, is not satisfied with what he sees, and smashes the mirror. He is later sent to the Tower, and a date for Bolingbroke's coronation is set. The Bishop of Carlisle, the Abbot of Westminster, Aumerle, and others, start a plot to get rid of the usurper.

V. i. The meeting and parting of Richard and his Queen as he is on his way to the Tower.

V. ii. York, in conversation with his wife, contrasts the reception of Bolingbroke and of Richard in London. He discovers by a chance Aumerle's part in the conspiracy, and departs hastily to inform Bolingbroke, in spite of his wife's protestations: she and Aumerle follow him.

V. iii. Bolingbroke comments on the ill-regulated life of his son. He hears Aumerle's story, listens to York's argument for his condemnation, and the Duchess's plea for his pardon. He spares Aumerle's life, and bids York set off at once to capture the plotters.

V. iv. Sir Pierce Exton reveals to his servant that Bolingbroke would welcome Richard's death: he proposes to kill Richard and win the royal favour.

V. v. Richard is shown in his solitary prison, weaving fantastic images on the theme of time. His faithful groom visits him and tells him of how his favourite horse seemed proud to bear Bolingbroke. The jailer orders the groom to go and places poisoned food before Richard. In desperation Richard attacks him. Exton and his servants enter and kill Richard after a furious conflict.

V. vi. Northumberland, Fitzwater, and Percy greet Bolingbroke in turn with news of victories on all sides. Finally Exton brings the coffined body of the dead Richard, and awaits his reward. But Bolingbroke banishes him from his presence, and proposes to undertake a voyage to the Holy Land to do penance for the crime that made his usurped crown secure.

THE PLAY ON THE SHAKESPEARIAN STAGE

The Elizabethan theatre was a very different affair from the modern one. The latter, a 'picture stage' in which the audience may be said to constitute the 'fourth wall' of a room, aims at illusion; the former, in which the stage was a platform thrust out among an audience, could not hope for this. The illustration on p. 6 makes a long explanation unnecessary. The platform constitutes the front or main stage; entrance was at the back (through any of several doors), not at the sides, so that some time elapsed between a character's appearance and his reaching the front of the stage. The building at the rear had a gallery above, which served for walls of a city, balcony of a room, &c. Below were curtains which, when drawn back, served to provide a rear or inner stage. As there was no means of closing the outer stage, scenes which had to be disclosed or hidden took place on this inner stage. There was little approximation to scenery, but plenty of movable properties (e.g. a 'mossy bank').

Most of the scenes in *The Tragedy of Richard the Second* call for the use of the main or outer stage: it is easier to list those that do not than those that do. In some scenes either the inner or the outer stage would be suitable. For instance, scene ii of Act I could be placed on either, but the fact that Gaunt is leaving *at once* for Coventry and the Duchess of Gloucester for Plashy makes it likely that the scene is thought of as taking place in a hall rather than in some private room: the outer stage would probably therefore be more suitable. In Act II, scene i, the number of actors involved would seem to call for the use of the main stage; but Gaunt's bed might easily be placed well towards the inner stage or actually on it. Scene ii of Act II might take place on the inner stage, as also scene iv of Act I and the last few lines of Act IV, scene i, where the conspirators put their heads together: but there is no *necessity* for locating these scenes there. On the other hand the use of the inner stage would be a distinct advantage in part of scene iii of Act I, where the king 'withdraws' to confer for a little with his council, and in scene v of Act V, where Richard is shown in prison. It could be used to good purpose in scene iii of Act V also, where Bolingbroke and Aumerle are alone and where York and his Duchess in turn pound upon the doors from 'within'.

The balcony would be called into use in Act III, scene iii, where Richard, Carlisle, and others 'enter on the walls' and talk to those below. It might also be used to swell the pageant of the abdication in Act IV, scene i.

Stage necessity directs the play for a moment in Act II, scene i, when, in order to save starting up a new scene, Shakespeare simply has Gaunt's bed removed—a most unlikely proceeding with a dying man! Similarly, for theatrical convenience, he leaves the Bishop of Carlisle among his friends, unattended, although he has just been put under arrest. Stage convention rather than necessity determines Bolingbroke's direction 'March sadly after' in scene vi of Act v; the coffin, being really empty, could have been left; but Shakespeare makes an excuse to clear the stage.

An interesting use of stage furniture is to be noted in Act III, scene iv, where the Queen says 'Let's step intc the shadow of these trees'. Apparently the 'trees' are the same as the 'dangling apricocks' which the under-gardener is to 'bind up'.

NOTES ON DRAMATIS PERSONAE

(See also the Summary of Richard II's reign above)

King Richard the Second, born 1367, son of the Black Prince, the eldest son of Edward III, who died in 1376. Thus Richard succeeded to the throne at his grandfather's death in 1377.

John of Gaunt, Duke of Lancaster, born 1340, fourth son of Edward III, whose second son Lionel had died in 1368. Gaunt was not historically the great figure that Shakespeare portrays in the year of his death, 1398.

Edmund of Langley, Duke of York, born 1341, fifth son of Edward III; an unambitious man who took little part in politics; died 1402.

Henry, surnamed *Bolingbroke*, &c., born 1367, eldest son of Gaunt; succeeded Richard II 1399, and reigned till 1413; father of Henry V, born 1387.

Duke of Aumerle, Earl of Rutland, York's eldest (but not really his only) son; killed at Agincourt 1415.

Thomas Mowbray, Duke of Norfolk. As governor of Calais in 1397 received into custody the Duke of Gloucester, seventh son of Edward III and youngest of Richard's uncles.

Duke of Surrey and the *Earl of Salisbury* afterwards took part in a plot against Henry IV and were beheaded 1400. Surrey had succeeded Norfolk as Earl Marshal.

Bushy and *Green* were appointed in 1398 to a Commission with four other commoners and twelve peers which was exercising all the powers of Parliament.

Earl of Northumberland, head of the Percy family and the most powerful lord in England.

Henry Percy, born 1364 and so a contemporary of Bolingbroke, to whose son he is made a rival in *1 Henry IV*.

Queen Isabella, see under 1396 in table above. Shakespeare is in fact creating a new character.

Duchess of Gloucester, sister-in-law of Bolingbroke, to whom she appeals in Act I, scene ii.

Duchess of York, second wife of York, whose first wife (died 1394) was really mother of Aumerle. This Duchess was Richard's niece by birth and his aunt by marriage!

DRAMATIS PERSONAE

KING RICHARD THE SECOND.

JOHN OF GAUNT, Duke of Lancaster, } Uncles to the King.
EDMUND OF LANGLEY, Duke of York, }

HENRY, surnamed BOLINGBROKE, Duke of Hereford, Son to John of Gaunt; afterwards King Henry IV.

DUKE OF AUMERLE, Son to the Duke of York.

THOMAS MOWBRAY, Duke of Norfolk.

DUKE OF SURREY.

EARL OF SALISBURY.

LORD BERKELEY.

BUSHY, }
BAGOT, } Servants to King Richard.
GREEN, }

EARL OF NORTHUMBERLAND.

HENRY PERCY, surnamed Hotspur, his Son.

LORD ROSS.

LORD WILLOUGHBY.

LORD FITZWATER.

BISHOP OF CARLISLE.

ABBOT OF WESTMINSTER.

LORD MARSHAL.

SIR PIERCE OF EXTON.

SIR STEPHEN SCROOP.

Captain of a Band of Welshmen.

QUEEN TO KING RICHARD.

DUCHESS OF GLOUCESTER.

DUCHESS OF YORK.

Lady attending on the Queen.

Lords, Heralds, Officers, Soldiers, Gardeners, Keeper, Messenger, Groom, and other Attendants.

SCENE—*Dispersedly in England and Wales.*

Glossarial notes dealing with words and phrases, and paraphrases of difficult passages, are given at the foot of the page where such seem necessary to keep the sense running. Other notes are printed in the commentary at the end. The sign [N] *in the footnotes indicates that a further note on the same line will be found in the commentary.*

THE TRAGEDY OF
KING RICHARD THE SECOND

ACT I

Scene I. London. A Room in the Palace

Enter KING RICHARD, *attended*; JOHN OF GAUNT, *and other* Nobles.

K. Richard. Old John of Gaunt, time-honour'd Lancaster,
Hast thou, according to thy oath and band,
Brought hither Henry Hereford thy bold son,
Here to make good the boisterous late appeal,
Which then our leisure would not let us hear, 5
Against the Duke of Norfolk, Thomas Mowbray?
Gaunt. I have, my liege.
K. Richard. Tell me, moreover, hast thou sounded him,
If he appeal the duke on ancient malice,
Or worthily, as a good subject should, 10
On some known ground of treachery in him?
Gaunt. As near as I could sift him on that argument,
On some apparent danger seen in him
Aim'd at your highness, no inveterate malice.
K. Richard. Then call them to our presence: face to face,
And frowning brow to brow, ourselves will hear 16
The accuser and the accused freely speak:
[*Exeunt some* Attendants.

2 **band:** bond. 3 **Hereford:** probably to be scanned and pronounced, as it was often spelt, Herford; so elsewhere. 4 **appeal:** accusation of treason which the accuser was bound under penalty to prove. So, as verb, = accuse (l. 9). 9 **ancient malice:** personal quarrel of long standing. 12 **sift him:** get to the bottom of his thoughts. **argument:** theme. 13 **apparent:** manifest.

High-stomach'd are they both, and full of ire,
In rage deaf as the sea, hasty as fire.

Re-enter Attendants, *with* BOLINGBROKE *and* MOWBRAY.

Bolingbroke. Many years of happy days befall 20
My gracious sovereign, my most loving liege!
Mowbray. Each day still better other's happiness;
Until the heavens, envying earth's good hap,
Add an immortal title to your crown!
K. Richard. We thank you both: yet one but flatters us,
As well appeareth by the cause you come, 26
Namely, to appeal each other of high treason.
Cousin of Hereford, what dost thou object
Against the Duke of Norfolk, Thomas Mowbray?
Bolingbroke. First,—heaven be the record to my speech!—
In the devotion of a subject's love, 31
Tendering the precious safety of my prince,
And free from other misbegotten hate,
Come I appellant to this princely presence.
Now, Thomas Mowbray, do I turn to thee, 35
And mark my greeting well; for what I speak
My body shall make good upon this earth,
Or my divine soul answer it in heaven.
Thou art a traitor and a miscreant;
Too good to be so and too bad to live, 40
Since the more fair and crystal is the sky,
The uglier seem the clouds that in it fly.

18 **high-stomach'd:** of proud courage. **ire:** anger. 23 **hap:** fortune (in having you as king). 26 **come:** come on. 30 **be the record to:** witness the truth of. 32 **tendering:** holding dear. 33 **other misbegotten hate:** he 'appeals' Mowbray not from personal malice but through loyalty. 37–8 Either I shall win, and so be proved right, or I shall die, and my soul be judged in heaven. 39 **miscreant:** villain (originally 'unbeliever'). 41 **too good:** men of his birth and position should be above treachery.

Once more, the more to aggravate the note,
With a foul traitor's name stuff I thy throat;
And wish, so please my sovereign, ere I move, 45
What my tongue speaks, my right drawn sword may prove.

Mowbray. Let not my cold words here accuse my zeal:
'Tis not the trial of a woman's war,
The bitter clamour of two eager tongues,
Can arbitrate this cause betwixt us twain; 50
The blood is hot that must be cool'd for this:
Yet can I not of such tame patience boast
As to be hush'd and nought at all to say.
First, the fair reverence of your highness curbs me
From giving reins and spurs to my free speech; 55
Which else would post until it had return'd
These terms of treason doubled down his throat.
Setting aside his high blood's royalty,
And let him be no kinsman to my liege,
I do defy him, and I spit at him; 60
Call him a slanderous coward and a villain:
Which to maintain I would allow him odds,
And meet him, were I tied to run afoot
Even to the frozen ridges of the Alps,
Or any other ground inhabitable, 65
Wherever Englishman durst set his foot.
Meantime let this defend my loyalty:
By all my hopes, most falsely doth he lie.

Bolingbroke. Pale trembling coward, there I throw my gage,
Disclaiming here the kindred of the king; 70
And lay aside my high blood's royalty,

43 **aggravate the note:** add to the insult. [*N*]. 46 **right:** rightly. 47 **accuse my zeal:** make me appear half-hearted. 54 **fair reverence:** seemly respect. 56 **post:** travel quickly. 59 **let him be:** suppose he were. 63 **tied:** obliged. 65 **inhabitable:** uninhabitable (opposite of habitable).

Which fear, not reverence, makes thee to except:
If guilty dread have left thee so much strength
As to take up mine honour's pawn, then stoop:
By that, and all the rites of knighthood else, 75
Will I make good against thee, arm to arm,
What I have spoke, or thou canst worse devise.

Mowbray. I take it up; and by that sword I swear,
Which gently laid my knighthood on my shoulder,
I'll answer thee in any fair degree, 80
Or chivalrous design of knightly trial:
And when I mount, alive may I not light,
If I be traitor or unjustly fight!

K. Richard. What doth our cousin lay to Mowbray's charge?
It must be great that can inherit us 85
So much as of a thought of ill in him.

Bolingbroke. Look, what I speak, my life shall prove it true;
That Mowbray hath receiv'd eight thousand nobles
In name of lendings for your highness' soldiers,
The which he hath detain'd for lewd employments, 90
Like a false traitor and injurious villain.
Besides I say and will in battle prove,
Or here or elsewhere to the furthest verge
That ever was survey'd by English eye,
That all the treasons for these eighteen years 95
Complotted and contrived in this land,
Fetch from false Mowbray their first head and spring.

72 **except:** take exception to, i.e. make an excuse of. 74 **honour's pawn:** i.e. his glove, thrown down as pledge. 77 **or:** or any other charge you can invent. 80–1 I will meet you in any fair trial arranged according to the code of chivalry. 85 **inherit:** make us possess. (Usually = possess, in Shakespeare.) 88 **nobles:** coin worth 20 groats, i.e. 6*s.* 8*d.* 89 **lendings:** money given to disburse for others—here, the English garrison at Calais. 90 **lewd:** base.

Further I say and further will maintain
Upon his bad life to make all this good,
That he did plot the Duke of Gloucester's death, 100
Suggest his soon-believing adversaries,
And consequently, like a traitor coward,
Sluic'd out his innocent soul through streams of blood:
Which blood, like sacrificing Abel's, cries,
Even from the tongueless caverns of the earth, 105
To me for justice and rough chastisement;
And, by the glorious worth of my descent,
This arm shall do it, or this life be spent.
K. Richard. How high a pitch his resolution soars!
Thomas of Norfolk, what sayst thou to this? 110
Mowbray. O! let my sovereign turn away his face
And bid his ears a little while be deaf,
Till I have told this slander of his blood
How God and good men hate so foul a liar.
K. Richard. Mowbray, impartial are our eyes and ears:
Were he my brother, nay, my kingdom's heir,— 116
As he is but my father's brother's son,—
Now, by my sceptre's awe I make a vow,
Such neighbour nearness to our sacred blood
Should nothing privilege him, nor partialize 120
The unstooping firmness of my upright soul.
He is our subject, Mowbray; so art thou:
Free speech and fearless I to thee allow.
Mowbray. Then, Bolingbroke, as low as to thy heart,
Through the false passage of thy throat, thou liest. 125
Three parts of that receipt I had for Calais

101 **suggest:** incite. Usually = tempt (cf. III. iv. 75). 102 **consequently:** after that (in time, *not* as a result of). 109 **pitch:** in falconry, height to which a hawk soars before descending on its prey. 113 **slander of his blood:** disgrace to the royal blood he (Hereford) bears. 120 **partialize:** make partial. [*N*]. 126 **receipt:** sum received.

Disburs'd I duly to his highness' soldiers;
The other part reserv'd I by consent,
For that my sovereign liege was in my debt
Upon remainder of a dear account, 130
Since last I went to France to fetch his queen.
Now swallow down that lie. For Gloucester's death,
I slew him not; but to mine own disgrace
Neglected my sworn duty in that case.
For you, my noble Lord of Lancaster, 135
The honourable father to my foe,
Once did I lay an ambush for your life,
A trespass that doth vex my grieved soul;
But ere I last receiv'd the sacrament
I did confess it, and exactly begg'd 140
Your Grace's pardon, and I hope I had it.
This is my fault: as for the rest appeal'd,
It issues from the rancour of a villain,
A recreant and most degenerate traitor;
Which in myself I boldly will defend, 145
And interchangeably hurl down my gage
Upon this overweening traitor's foot,
To prove myself a loyal gentleman
Even in the best blood chamber'd in his bosom.
In haste whereof, most heartily I pray 150
Your highness to assign our trial day.

K. Richard. Wrath-kindled gentlemen, be rul'd by me;
Let's purge this choler without letting blood:
This we prescribe, though no physician;
Deep malice makes too deep incision: 155

130 **Upon remainder . . . account:** as the balance of the heavy debt. [*N*]. 140 **exactly:** in precise detail, fully. 142 **appeal'd:** of which I am accused. 144 **recreant:** cowardly (one who admits defeat, and so guilt, in trial by combat). 145 **in myself:** in my own person. 146 **interchangeably:** in turn (cf. l. 69). 149 **chamber'd:** contained. 153 **purge this choler:** get rid of this anger. [*N*].

Forget, forgive; conclude and be agreed,
Our doctors say this is no month to bleed.
Good uncle, let this end where it begun;
We'll calm the Duke of Norfolk, you your son.
Gaunt. To be a make-peace shall become my age: 160
Throw down, my son, the Duke of Norfolk's gage.
K. Richard. And, Norfolk, throw down his.
Gaunt. When, Harry, when?
Obedience bids I should not bid again.
K. Richard. Norfolk, throw down, we bid; there is no boot.
Mowbray. Myself I throw, dread sovereign, at thy foot.
My life thou shalt command, but not my shame: 166
The one my duty owes; but my fair name,—
Despite of death that lives upon my grave,—
To dark dishonour's use thou shalt not have.
I am disgrac'd, impeach'd, and baffled here, 170
Pierc'd to the soul with slander's venom'd spear,
The which no balm can cure but his heart-blood
Which breath'd this poison.
K. Richard. Rage must be withstood:
Give me his gage: lions make leopards tame.
Mowbray. Yea, but not change his spots: take but my shame, 175
And I resign my gage. My dear dear lord,
The purest treasure mortal times afford
Is spotless reputation; that away,
Men are but gilded loam or painted clay.
A jewel in a ten-times-barr'd-up chest 180

156 **conclude:** come to final settlement. 164 **no boot:** no help; possibly, 'no advantage in refusing'. 165 **Myself:** as opposed to Bolingbroke's gage, which he still holds. 167–9 Duty makes me put my life at your disposal; but my reputation, which lives after me, is not yours to abuse. [*N*]. 170 **impeach'd:** accused, baffled; shamefully disgraced. [*N*]. 177 **mortal times:** the span of human life.

Is a bold spirit in a loyal breast.
Mine honour is my life; both grow in one;
Take honour from me, and my life is done:
Then, dear my liege, mine honour let me try;
In that I live and for that will I die. 185

K. Richard. Cousin, throw down your gage: do you begin.

Bolingbroke. O! God defend my soul from such deep sin.
Shall I seem crest-fall'n in my father's sight,
Or with pale beggar-fear impeach my height
Before this out-dar'd dastard? Ere my tongue 190
Shall wound mine honour with such feeble wrong,
Or sound so base a parle, my teeth shall tear
The slavish motive of recanting fear,
And spit it bleeding in his high disgrace,
Where shame doth harbour, even in Mowbray's face. 195

[*Exit* GAUNT.

K. Richard. We were not born to sue, but to command:
Which since we cannot do to make you friends,
Be ready, as your lives shall answer it,
At Coventry, upon Saint Lambert's day:
There shall your swords and lances arbitrate 200
The swelling difference of your settled hate:
Since we cannot atone you, we shall see
Justice design the victor's chivalry.
Marshal, command our officers-at-arms 204
Be ready to direct these home alarms. [*Exeunt.*

189 **impeach my height:** lay myself open to the charge of not behaving as one of noble birth and position should. [*N*]. 191 **feeble wrong:** insult done to his honour through his weakness. 192 **sound . . . a parle:** ask for a truce. 193 **motive:** that which moves or expresses, the instrument. 194 **his:** its. This use of it would disgrace it still further. 202 **atone:** make at one, reconcile. 203 **design the victor's chivalry:** indicate the true knight by making him win.

Scene II. The Same. A Room in the Duke of Lancaster's Palace

Enter GAUNT *and* DUCHESS OF GLOUCESTER

Gaunt. Alas! the part I had in Woodstock's blood
Doth more solicit me than your exclaims,
To stir against the butchers of his life.
But since correction lieth in those hands
Which made the fault that we cannot correct, 5
Put we our quarrel to the will of heaven;
Who, when they see the hours ripe on earth,
Will rain hot vengeance on offenders' heads.
Duchess. Finds brotherhood in thee no sharper spur?
Hath love in thy old blood no living fire? 10
Edward's seven sons, whereof thyself art one,
Were as seven vials of his sacred blood,
Or seven fair branches springing from one root:
Some of those seven are dried by nature's course,
Some of those branches by the Destinies cut; 15
But Thomas, my dear lord, my life, my Gloucester,
One vial full of Edward's sacred blood,
One flourishing branch of his most royal root,
Is crack'd, and all the precious liquor spilt;
Is hack'd down, and his summer leaves all vaded, 20
By envy's hand and murder's bloody axe.
Ah, Gaunt! his blood was thine: that bed, that womb,
That metal, that self-mould, that fashion'd thee
Made him a man; and though thou liv'st and breath'st,
Yet art thou slain in him: thou dost consent 25

2 **solicit:** move. 4–5 The king should inflict punishment in this matter—but he himself is the criminal. (Deliberately vague.) 9 Cannot your dead brother find in you a keener avenger than that? 12 **vials:** phials. 15 **by the Destinies cut:** naturally, by the accidents incidental to human life. [*N*]. 20 **vaded:** faded. 21 **envy:** malice. 23 **self-mould:** same mould; cf. 'self-same'. 25 **consent:** agree to, with the idea of complicity.

In some large measure to thy father's death
In that thou seest thy wretched brother die,
Who was the model of thy father's life.
Call it not patience, Gaunt; it is despair:
In suffering thus thy brother to be slaughter'd 30
Thou show'st the naked pathway to thy life,
Teaching stern murder how to butcher thee:
That which in mean men we entitle patience
Is pale cold cowardice in noble breasts.
What shall I say? to safeguard thine own life, 35
The best way is to venge my Gloucester's death.

Gaunt. God's is the quarrel; for God's substitute,
His deputy anointed in his sight,
Hath caus'd his death: the which if wrongfully,
Let heaven revenge, for I may never lift 40
An angry arm against his minister.

Duchess. Where then, alas! may I complain myself?

Gaunt. To God, the widow's champion and defence.

Duchess. Why then, I will. Farewell, old Gaunt.
Thou go'st to Coventry, there to behold 45
Our cousin Hereford and fell Mowbray fight:
O! sit my husband's wrongs on Hereford's spear,
That it may enter butcher Mowbray's breast.
Or if misfortune miss the first career,
Be Mowbray's sins so heavy in his bosom 50
That they may break his foaming courser's back,
And throw the rider headlong in the lists,
A caitiff recreant to my cousin Hereford!
Farewell, old Gaunt: thy sometimes brother's wife

28 **model:** image, copy. 30 **suffering:** passively allowing. 31 **naked pathway:** the way to be open. 33 **mean:** of low degree. 42 **complain myself:** cf. *me plaindre*, and see 'retire', II. ii. 46, IV. i. 96. 49 If ill luck does not befall (Mowbray) in the first charge. **career:** charge at full speed on horseback. 53 **caitiff recreant:** wretched yielder, and retractor of words. 54 **thy sometimes brother's wife:** wife of him who was once thy brother. [*N*].

With her companion grief must end her life. 55

Gaunt. Sister, farewell; I must to Coventry.
As much good stay with thee as go with me!

Duchess. Yet one word more. Grief boundeth where it falls,
Not with the empty hollowness, but weight:
I take my leave before I have begun, 60
For sorrow ends not when it seemeth done.
Commend me to my brother, Edmund York.
Lo! this is all: nay, yet depart not so;
Though this be all, do not so quickly go;
I shall remember more. Bid him—ah, what?— 65
With all good speed at Plashy visit me.
Alack! and what shall good old York there see
But empty lodgings and unfurnish'd walls,
Unpeopled offices, untrodden stones?
And what hear there for welcome but my groans? 70
Therefore commend me; let him not come there,
To seek out sorrow that dwells every where.
Desolate, desolate will I hence, and die:
The last leave of thee takes my weeping eye. [*Exeunt.*

Scene III. OPEN SPACE, NEAR COVENTRY. LISTS SET OUT, AND A THRONE. HERALDS, &c., ATTENDING

Enter the Lord Marshal *and* AUMERLE.

Marshal. My Lord Aumerle, is Harry Hereford arm'd?

Aumerle. Yea, at all points, and longs to enter in.

Marshal. The Duke of Norfolk, sprightfully and bold,
Stays but the summons of the appellant's trumpet.

58–9 A ball rebounds because of its lightness; my grief returns (and makes me speak again) because of its weight and force. 68 **unfurnish'd**: without hangings, or arras. 69 **offices**: parts of a mansion occupied by the servants.
3 **bold**: boldly.

Aumerle. Why then, the champions are prepar'd, and stay 5
For nothing but his majesty's approach.

Flourish. Enter KING RICHARD, *who takes his seat on his Throne*; GAUNT, BUSHY, BAGOT, GREEN, *and others, who take their places. A trumpet is sounded, and answered by another trumpet within. Then enter* MOWBRAY, *in armour, defendant, preceded by a* Herald.

K. Richard. Marshal, demand of yonder champion
The cause of his arrival here in arms:
Ask him his name, and orderly proceed
To swear him in the justice of his cause. 10

Marshal. In God's name, and the king's, say who thou art,
And why thou com'st thus knightly clad in arms,
Against what man thou com'st, and what thy quarrel.
Speak truly, on thy knighthood and thine oath;
As so defend thee heaven and thy valour! 15

Mowbray. My name is Thomas Mowbray, Duke of Norfolk,
Who hither come engaged by my oath,—
Which God defend a knight should violate!—
Both to defend my loyalty and truth
To God, my king, and my succeeding issue, 20
Against the Duke of Hereford that appeals me;
And, by the grace of God and this mine arm,
To prove him, in defending of myself,
A traitor to my God, my king, and me:
And as I truly fight, defend me heaven! 25

[*He takes his seat.*

10 **swear him in**: make him take an oath as to. 18 **defend**: forbid.

Trumpet sounds. Enter BOLINGBROKE, *appellant, in armour, preceded by a* Herald.

K. Richard. Marshal, ask yonder knight in arms,
Both who he is and why he cometh hither
Thus plated in habiliments of war;
And formally, according to our law,
Depose him in the justice of his cause. 30

Marshal. What is thy name? and wherefore com'st thou hither,
Before King Richard in his royal lists?
Against whom comest thou? and what's thy quarrel?
Speak like a true knight, so defend thee heaven!

Bolingbroke. Harry of Hereford, Lancaster, and Derby, 35
Am I; who ready here do stand in arms,
To prove by God's grace and my body's valour,
In lists, on Thomas Mowbray, Duke of Norfolk,
That he's a traitor foul and dangerous,
To God of heaven, King Richard, and to me: 40
And as I truly fight, defend me heaven!

Marshal. On pain of death, no person be so bold
Or daring-hardy as to touch the lists,
Except the marshal and such officers
Appointed to direct these fair designs. 45

Bolingbroke. Lord marshal, let me kiss my sovereign's hand,
And bow my knee before his majesty:
For Mowbray and myself are like two men
That vow a long and weary pilgrimage;
Then let us take a ceremonious leave 50
And loving farewell of our several friends.

Marshal. The appellant in all duty greets your highness,
And craves to kiss your hand and take his leave.

30 **Depose**: make him swear under oath (parallel to 'swear', l. 10). 51 **several**: respective.

K. Richard. [*Descends from his throne.*] We will descend and fold him in our arms.
Cousin of Hereford, as thy cause is right, 55
So be thy fortune in this royal fight!
Farewell, my blood, which if to-day thou shed,
Lament we may, but not revenge thee dead.

Bolingbroke. O! let no noble eye profane a tear
For me, if I be gor'd with Mowbray's spear. 60
As confident as is the falcon's flight
Against a bird, do I with Mowbray fight.
My loving lord, I take my leave of you;
Of you, my noble cousin, Lord Aumerle;
Not sick, although I have to do with death, 65
But lusty, young, and cheerly drawing breath.
Lo! as at English feasts, so I regreet
The daintiest last, to make the end most sweet:
O thou, the earthly author of my blood,
Whose youthful spirit, in me regenerate, 70
Doth with a two-fold vigour lift me up
To reach at victory above my head,
Add proof unto mine armour with thy prayers,
And with thy blessings steel my lance's point,
That it may enter Mowbray's waxen coat, 75
And furbish new the name of John a Gaunt,
Even in the lusty haviour of his son.

Gaunt. God in thy good cause make thee prosperous!
Be swift like lightning in the execution;
And let thy blows, doubly redoubled, 80
Fall like amazing thunder on the casque

59 **profane:** waste (shed idly on an unworthy object). 66 **cheerly:** cheerily. 67 **regreet:** greet. [*N*]. 70 **regenerate:** living again. 73 **proof:** strength, power to resist (cf. 'shower-proof'). 75 **waxen:** the anticipatory or proleptic use = which will seem like wax. 76 **furbish:** give lustre to. 77 **haviour:** carriage, deportment. 81 **amazing:** producing bewilderment. **casque:** helmet.

Of thy adverse pernicious enemy:
Rouse up thy youthful blood, be valiant and live.
Bolingbroke. Mine innocency and Saint George to thrive!
[*He takes his seat.*
Mowbray. [*Rising.*] However God or fortune cast my lot,
There lives or dies, true to King Richard's throne, 86
A loyal, just, and upright gentleman.
Never did captive with a freer heart
Cast off his chains of bondage and embrace
His golden uncontroll'd enfranchisement, 90
More than my dancing soul doth celebrate
This feast of battle with mine adversary.
Most mighty liege, and my companion peers,
Take from my mouth the wish of happy years;
As gentle and as jocund as to jest, 95
Go I to fight: truth has a quiet breast.
K. Richard. Farewell, my lord: securely I espy
Virtue with valour couched in thine eye.
Order the trial, marshal, and begin.
[*The* KING *and the* Lords *return to their seats.*
Marshal. Harry of Hereford, Lancaster, and Derby, 100
Receive thy lance; and God defend the right!
Bolingbroke. [*Rising.*] Strong as a tower in hope, I cry 'amen'.
Marshal. [*To an* Officer.] Go bear this lance to Thomas, Duke of Norfolk.
First Herald. Harry of Hereford, Lancaster, and Derby,
Stands here for God, his sovereign, and himself, 105
On pain to be found false and recreant,
To prove the Duke of Norfolk, Thomas Mowbray,

84 May my innocence and Saint George be my assurance of success, make me to thrive. 95 **jest:** merriment or entertainment, not necessarily of words. 97 **securely:** confidently (couched). 99 **Order:** make the arrangements for. 106 **On pain to be found:** at the risk of being found (cf. l. 153).

A traitor to his God, his king, and him;
And dares him to set forward to the fight.

Second Herald. Here standeth Thomas Mowbray, Duke of Norfolk, 110
On pain to be found false and recreant,
Both to defend himself and to approve
Henry of Hereford, Lancaster, and Derby,
To God, his sovereign, and to him, disloyal;
Courageously and with a free desire, 115
Attending but the signal to begin.

Marshal. Sound, trumpets; and set forward, combatants.
[*A charge sounded.*
Stay, stay, the king hath thrown his warder down.

K. Richard. Let them lay by their helmets and their spears,
And both return back to their chairs again: 120
Withdraw with us; and let the trumpets sound
While we return these dukes what we decree.
[*A long flourish.*
[*To the Combatants.*] Draw near,
And list what with our council we have done.
For that our kingdom's earth should not be soil'd 125
With that dear blood which it hath fostered;
And for our eyes do hate the dire aspect
Of civil wounds plough'd up with neighbours' swords;
And for we think the eagle-winged pride
Of sky-aspiring and ambitious thoughts, 130
With rival-hating envy, set on you
To wake our peace, which in our country's cradle
Draws the sweet infant breath of gentle sleep;

116 **Attending**: awaiting. 118 **warder**: a kind of truncheon carried by the person who presided at these single combats. To throw it down was a signal to stop. 122 **While**: till. **return**: answer the appeal of. 124 **list**: hear. 127 **for**: because. 131 **set on you**: set you on.

Which so rous'd up with boist'rous untun'd drums,
With harsh-resounding trumpets' dreadful bray, 135
And grating shock of wrathful iron arms,
Might from our quiet confines fright fair peace
And make us wade even in our kindred's blood:
Therefore, we banish you our territories:
You, cousin Hereford, upon pain of life, 140
Till twice five summers have enrich'd our fields,
Shall not regreet our fair dominions,
But tread the stranger paths of banishment.

Bolingbroke. Your will be done: this must my comfort be,
That sun that warms you here shall shine on me; 145
And those his golden beams to you here lent
Shall point on me and gild my banishment.

K. Richard. Norfolk, for thee remains a heavier doom,
Which I with some unwillingness pronounce:
The sly slow hours shall not determinate 150
The dateless limit of thy dear exile;
The hopeless word of 'never to return'
Breathe I against thee, upon pain of life.

Mowbray. A heavy sentence, my most sovereign liege,
And all unlook'd for from your highness' mouth: 155
A dearer merit, not so deep a maim
As to be cast forth in the common air,
Have I deserved at your highness' hands.
The language I have learn'd these forty years,
My native English, now I must forego; 160
And now my tongue's use is to me no more
Than an unstringed viol or a harp,
Or like a cunning instrument cas'd up,

143 **stranger**: foreign. 150 **sly**: passing with stealthy foot. **determinate**: put a limit to, settle. 151 **dear**: grievous, that affects deeply; cf. I. i. 130. 156 **dearer merit**: better reward; merit = that which is merited. 162 **viol**: a kind of violin. 163 **cunning**: requiring 'cunning', i.e. skill, to play it.

Or, being open, put into his hands
That knows no touch to tune the harmony: 165
Within my mouth you have engaol'd my tongue,
Doubly portcullis'd with my teeth and lips;
And dull, unfeeling, barren ignorance
Is made my gaoler to attend on me.
I am too old to fawn upon a nurse, 170
Too far in years to be a pupil now:
What is thy sentence then but speechless death,
Which robs my tongue from breathing native breath?

K. Richard. It boots thee not to be compassionate:
After our sentence plaining comes too late. 175

Mowbray. Then, thus I turn me from my country's light,
To dwell in solemn shades of endless night. [*Retiring.*

K. Richard. Return again, and take an oath with thee.
Lay on our royal sword your banish'd hands;
Swear by the duty that you owe to God— 180
Our part therein we banish with yourselves—
To keep the oath that we administer:
You never shall,—so help you truth and God!—
Embrace each other's love in banishment;
Nor never look upon each other's face; 185
Nor never write, regreet, nor reconcile
This low'ring tempest of your home-bred hate;
Nor never by advised purpose meet
To plot, contrive, or complot any ill
'Gainst us, our state, our subjects, or our land. 190

Bolingbroke. I swear.

Mowbray. And I, to keep all this.

167 **portcullis'd:** shut in, fortified. 172 **speechless death:** death with no further chance of speaking. 174 **compassionate:** probably = expressing or displaying emotion (cf. 'passionate'), but possibly = deeply moving, pathetic. [*N*]. 178 **take:** i.e. into exile. 179 **sword:** the blade and hilt forming a kind of cross. 188 **advised:** deliberate. 189 **complot:** see note to I. i. 96.

Bolingbroke. Norfolk, so far, as to mine enemy:—
By this time, had the king permitted us,
One of our souls had wander'd in the air, 195
Banish'd this frail sepulchre of our flesh,
As now our flesh is banish'd from this land:
Confess thy treasons ere thou fly the realm;
Since thou hast far to go, bear not along
The clogging burden of a guilty soul. 200

Mowbray. No, Bolingbroke: if ever I were traitor,
My name be blotted from the book of life,
And I from heaven banish'd as from hence!
But what thou art, God, thou, and I do know;
And all too soon, I fear, the king shall rue. 205
Farewell, my liege. Now no way can I stray;
Save back to England, all the world's my way. [*Exit.*

K. Richard. Uncle, even in the glasses of thine eyes
I see thy grieved heart: thy sad aspect
Hath from the number of his banish'd years 210
Pluck'd four away.—[*To* BOL.] Six frozen winters spent,
Return with welcome home from banishment.

Bolingbroke. How long a time lies in one little word!
Four lagging winters and four wanton springs
End in a word: such is the breath of kings. 215

Gaunt. I thank my liege, that in regard of me
He shortens four years of my son's exile;
But little vantage shall I reap thereby:
For, ere the six years that he hath to spend
Can change their moons and bring their times about, 220
My oil-dried lamp and time-bewasted light
Shall be extinct with age and endless night;
My inch of taper will be burnt and done,

193 **so far**: if I may speak thus much to my enemy. 206 **stray**: go wrong. 208 **uncle**: i.e. Gaunt. **glasses**: the eyes mirror the heart. 220 **bring their times about**: bring round their seasons.

And blindfold death not let me see my son. 224
K. Richard. Why, uncle, thou hast many years to live.
Gaunt. But not a minute, king, that thou canst give:
Shorten my days thou canst with sullen sorrow,
And pluck nights from me, but not lend a morrow;
Thou canst help time to furrow me with age,
But stop no wrinkle in his pilgrimage; 230
Thy word is current with him for my death,
But dead, thy kingdom cannot buy my breath.
K. Richard. Thy son is banish'd upon good advice,
Whereto thy tongue a party-verdict gave:
Why at our justice seem'st thou then to lower? 235
Gaunt. Things sweet to taste prove in digestion sour.
You urg'd me as a judge; but I had rather
You would have bid me argue like a father.
O! had it been a stranger, not my child,
To smooth his fault I should have been more mild: 240
A partial slander sought I to avoid,
And in the sentence my own life destroy'd.
Alas! I look'd when some of you should say,
I was too strict to make mine own away;
But you gave leave to my unwilling tongue 245
Against my will to do myself this wrong.
K. Richard. Cousin, farewell; and, uncle, bid him so:
Six years we banish him, and he shall go.
[*Flourish. Exeunt* KING RICHARD *and Train.*
Aumerle. Cousin, farewell: what presence must not know,

224 **blindfold:** either (1) blind, and so striking at random, or (2) involving blindness, i.e. in the dead. 231 **current with him:** time accepts it as valid; a figure from coinage. 233 **upon good advice:** after due consideration (cf. l. 188). 234 **party-verdict:** decision in which you joined. 235 **lower:** look gloomy. 241 **partial slander:** the reproach of favouritism. 243 **look'd when:** expected. 244 **to make mine own away:** in banishing my own (son). 249 **what presence . . . know:** what we cannot learn from you in person. [*N*].

From where you do remain let paper show. 250
Marshal. My lord, no leave take I; for I will ride,
As far as land will let me, by your side.
Gaunt. O! to what purpose dost thou hoard thy words,
That thou return'st no greeting to thy friends?
Bolingbroke. I have too few to take my leave of you,
When the tongue's office should be prodigal 256
To breathe the abundant dolour of the heart.
Gaunt. Thy grief is but thy absence for a time.
Bolingbroke. Joy absent, grief is present for that time.
Gaunt. What is six winters? they are quickly gone. 260
Bolingbroke. To men in joy; but grief makes one hour ten.
Gaunt. Call it a travel that thou tak'st for pleasure.
Bolingbroke. My heart will sigh when I miscall it so,
Which finds it an inforced pilgrimage.
Gaunt. The sullen passage of thy weary steps 265
Esteem as foil wherein thou art to set
The precious jewel of thy home return.
Bolingbroke. Nay, rather, every tedious stride I make
Will but remember me what a deal of world
I wander from the jewels that I love. 270
Must I not serve a long apprenticehood
To foreign passages, and in the end,
Having my freedom, boast of nothing else
But that I was a journeyman to grief?
Gaunt. All places that the eye of heaven visits 275
Are to a wise man ports and happy havens.
Teach thy necessity to reason thus;
There is no virtue like necessity.
Think not the king did banish thee,

256–7 **prodigal To breathe:** lavish in expressing (cf. l. 244). 258 **Thy grief:** either (1) grievance, or (2) sorrow, pain. [*N*]. 269 **remember:** remind (as very often). 272 **passages:** wanderings. [*N*]. 278 **There . . . necessity:** nothing has such compulsive 'virtue' or efficacy as necessity.

But thou the king. Woe doth the heavier sit, 280
Where it perceives it is but faintly borne.
Go, say I sent thee forth to purchase honour,
And not the king exil'd thee; or suppose
Devouring pestilence hangs in our air,
And thou art flying to a fresher clime. 285
Look, what thy soul holds dear, imagine it
To lie that way thou go'st, not whence thou com'st.
Suppose the singing birds musicians,
The grass whereon thou tread'st the presence strew'd,
The flowers fair ladies, and thy steps no more 290
Than a delightful measure or a dance;
For gnarling sorrow hath less power to bite
The man that mocks at it and sets it light.

Bolingbroke. O! who can hold a fire in his hand
By thinking on the frosty Caucasus? 295
Or cloy the hungry edge of appetite
By bare imagination of a feast?
Or wallow naked in December snow
By thinking on fantastic summer's heat?
O, no! the apprehension of the good 300
Gives but the greater feeling to the worse:
Fell sorrow's tooth doth never rankle more
Than when it bites, but lanceth not the sore.

Gaunt. Come, come, my son, I'll bring thee on thy way.
Had I thy youth and cause, I would not stay. 305

281 **faintly borne:** not manfully opposed. 282 **purchase:** acquire (not *by payment* only). 289 **presence:** presence chamber at court. **strew'd:** with rushes for carpet. 291 **measure:** stately dance. [*N*]. 292 **gnarling:** snarling. 293 **sets:** accounts. 299 **fantastic:** produced by the fantasy or imagination. 300 **apprehension:** conception. 'A vivid conception of a great thing which one lacks makes one more keenly sensitive to the bad things that we have to put up with' (Verity). 303 **lanceth:** cuts (as a necessary preliminary to its healing). [*N*]. 304 **bring:** accompany; cf. I. iv. 2.

Bolingbroke. Then, England's ground, farewell; sweet soil, adieu:
My mother, and my nurse, that bears me yet!
Where'er I wander, boast of this I can,
Though banish'd, yet a true-born Englishman. [*Exeunt.*

Scene IV. LONDON. A ROOM IN THE KING'S CASTLE

Enter KING RICHARD, BAGOT, *and* GREEN *at one door;* AUMERLE *at another.*

K. Richard. We did observe. Cousin Aumerle,
How far brought you high Hereford on his way?
Aumerle. I brought high Hereford, if you call him so,
But to the next highway, and there I left him.
K. Richard. And say, what store of parting tears were shed? 5
Aumerle. Faith, none for me; except the north-east wind,
Which then blew bitterly against our faces,
Awak'd the sleeping rheum, and so by chance
Did grace our hollow parting with a tear.
K. Richard. What said our cousin when you parted with him? 10
Aumerle. 'Farewell:'
And, for my heart disdained that my tongue
Should so profane the word, that taught me craft
To counterfeit oppression of such grief
That words seem'd buried in my sorrow's grave. 15
Marry, would the word 'farewell' have lengthen'd hours
And added years to his short banishment,

6 **for me:** on my part. 8 **Awak'd . . . rheum:** made my eyes water (rheum = cold moisture). 9 **hollow:** insincere. 13 **that:** that fact, i.e. his refusal to utter words he did not mean. 14–15 **To counterfeit . . . grave:** to pretend to be so weighed down with grief that words seem buried in my sorrow as in a grave. 16 **Marry:** by the Virgin Mary.

He should have had a volume of farewells;
But, since it would not, he had none of me.
K. Richard. He is our cousin, cousin; but 'tis doubt, 20
When time shall call him home from banishment,
Whether our kinsman come to see his friends.
Ourself and Bushy, Bagot here and Green,
Observ'd his courtship to the common people,
How he did seem to dive into their hearts 25
With humble and familiar courtesy,
What reverence he did throw away on slaves,
Wooing poor craftsmen with the craft of smiles
And patient underbearing of his fortune,
As 'twere to banish their affects with him. 30
Off goes his bonnet to an oyster-wench;
A brace of draymen bid God speed him well,
And had the tribute of his supple knee,
With 'Thanks, my countrymen, my loving friends;'
As were our England in reversion his, 35
And he our subjects' next degree in hope.
Green. Well, he is gone; and with him go these thoughts.
Now for the rebels which stand out in Ireland;
Expedient manage must be made, my liege,
Ere further leisure yield them further means 40
For their advantage and your highness' loss.
K. Richard. We will ourself in person to this war.
And, for our coffers with too great a court
And liberal largess are grown somewhat light,
We are enforc'd to farm our royal realm; 45
The revenue whereof shall furnish us

29 **underbearing**: enduring. 30 **banish their affects**: take their affections into banishment. 35 **As were . . . his**: as if he were legal heir to the throne. [*N*]. 37 **go these thoughts**: let us banish him from our minds. 39 **Expedient manage**: speedy arrangement. 44 **largess**: gifts (cf. IV. i. 282). 45 **farm**: let out on lease. [*N*].

For our affairs in hand. If that come short,
Our substitutes at home shall have blank charters;
Whereto, when they shall know what men are rich,
They shall subscribe them for large sums of gold, 50
And send them after to supply our wants;
For we will make for Ireland presently.

Enter BUSHY.

Bushy, what news?

Bushy. Old John of Gaunt is grievous sick, my lord,
Suddenly taken, and hath sent post-haste 55
To entreat your majesty visit him.

K. Richard. Where lies he?

Bushy. At Ely House.

K. Richard. Now, put it, God, in his physician's mind
To help him to his grave immediately! 60
The lining of his coffers shall make coats
To deck our soldiers for these Irish wars.
Come, gentlemen, let's all go visit him:
Pray God we may make haste, and come too late.

All. Amen. [*Exeunt.*

48 **blank charters**: the king's officers compelled rich men to sign as it were blank cheques and then filled in the amount payable as they chose. 50 **subscribe them**: put their names down. 52 **presently**: at once. 61 **lining**: contents, with a play on 'lining' and 'coats'. [*N*].

ACT II

Scene I. LONDON. AN APARTMENT IN ELY HOUSE

GAUNT *on a couch; the* DUKE OF YORK *and Others standing by him.*

Gaunt. Will the king come, that I may breathe my last
In wholesome counsel to his unstaid youth?
York. Vex not yourself, nor strive not with your breath;
For all in vain comes counsel to his ear.
Gaunt. O! but they say the tongues of dying men 5
Enforce attention like deep harmony:
Where words are scarce, they are seldom spent in vain,
For they breathe truth that breathe their words in pain.
He that no more must say is listen'd more
Than they whom youth and ease have taught to glose;
More are men's ends mark'd than their lives before: 11
The setting sun, and music at the close,
As the last taste of sweets, is sweetest last,
Writ in remembrance more than things long past:
Though Richard my life's counsel would not hear, 15
My death's sad tale may yet undeaf his ear.
York. No; it is stopp'd with other flattering sounds,
As praises of his state: then there are fond
Lascivious metres, to whose venom sound
The open ear of youth doth always listen: 20
Report of fashions in proud Italy,
Whose manners still our tardy apish nation
Limps after in base imitation.

10 **glose**: flatter, speak insincerely. 12 **music at the close**: the 'dying fall' or harmonious end of a piece of music. 16 **undeaf**: unstop. Cf. 'unhappied' (III. i. 10), 'unkiss' (V. i. 74). 17 **other flattering sounds**: other voices, which, unlike yours, are flattering. 18 **fond**: foolish. 19 **venom**: poisonous.

Where doth the world thrust forth a vanity,—
So it be new there's no respect how vile,— 25
That is not quickly buzz'd into his ears?
Then all too late comes counsel to be heard,
Where will doth mutiny with wit's regard.
Direct not him whose way himself will choose:
'Tis breath thou lack'st, and that breath wilt thou lose. 30

Gaunt. Methinks I am a prophet new inspir'd,
And thus expiring do foretell of him:
His rash fierce blaze of riot cannot last,
For violent fires soon burn out themselves;
Small showers last long, but sudden storms are short; 35
He tires betimes that spurs too fast betimes;
With eager feeding food doth choke the feeder:
Light vanity, insatiate cormorant,
Consuming means, soon preys upon itself.
This royal throne of kings, this scepter'd isle, 40
This earth of majesty, this seat of Mars,
This other Eden, demi-paradise,
This fortress built by Nature for herself
Against infection and the hand of war,
This happy breed of men, this little world, 45
This precious stone set in the silver sea,
Which serves it in the office of a wall,
Or as a moat defensive to a house,
Against the envy of less happier lands,
This blessed plot, this earth, this realm, this England, 50
This nurse, this teeming womb of royal kings,

25 **no respect:** no consideration. 28 **Where . . . regard:** where inclination refuses to follow the judgement of reason. [*N*]. 29 **whose way:** who will choose his own way for himself. 36 **betimes:** early. 39 **means:** its resources. 41 **of majesty:** fitted to be the abode of majesty. 44 **infection:** plague, corruption from abroad (moral and physical). 49 **envy:** malice (as commonly; cf. l. 62). [*N*].

Fear'd by their breed and famous by their birth,
Renowned for their deeds as far from home,—
For Christian service and true chivalry,—
As is the sepulchre in stubborn Jewry 55
Of the world's ransom, blessed Mary's Son:
This land of such dear souls, this dear, dear land,
Dear for her reputation through the world,
Is now leas'd out,—I die pronouncing it,—
Like to a tenement, or pelting farm: 60
England, bound in with the triumphant sea,
Whose rocky shore beats back the envious siege
Of watery Neptune, is now bound in with shame,
With inky blots, and rotten parchment bonds:
That England, that was wont to conquer others, 65
Hath made a shameful conquest of itself.
Ah! would the scandal vanish with my life,
How happy then were my ensuing death.

Enter KING RICHARD *and* QUEEN; AUMERLE, BUSHY, GREEN, BAGOT, ROSS, *and* WILLOUGHBY.

York. The king is come: deal mildly with his youth;
For young hot colts, being rag'd, do rage the more. 70
Queen. How fares our noble uncle, Lancaster?
K. Richard. What comfort, man? How is't with aged Gaunt?
Gaunt. O! how that name befits my composition;
Old Gaunt indeed, and gaunt in being old:
Within me grief hath kept a tedious fast; 75
And who abstains from meat that is not gaunt?
For sleeping England long time have I watch'd;
Watching breeds leanness, leanness is all gaunt.

52 **by their breed**: on account of their race. 55 **Jewry**: land of the Jews, Judea. [*N.*] 60 **pelting**: petty, paltry. For the idea, cf. I. iv. 45 and note. 68 **ensuing**: oncoming—without the idea of *consequence*. 70 **rag'd**: raged at. 73 **composition**: condition. 75 My grief has made me refrain from eating.

The pleasure that some fathers feed upon
Is my strict fast, I mean my children's looks; 80
And therein fasting hast thou made me gaunt.
Gaunt am I for the grave, gaunt as a grave,
Whose hollow womb inherits nought but bones.

K. Richard. Can sick men play so nicely with their names?

Gaunt. No; misery makes sport to mock itself: 85
Since thou dost seek to kill my name in me,
I mock my name, great king, to flatter thee.

K. Richard. Should dying men flatter with those that live?

Gaunt. No, no; men living flatter those that die.

K. Richard. Thou, now a-dying, sayst thou flatter'st me.

Gaunt. O, no! thou diest, though I the sicker be. 91

K. Richard. I am in health, I breathe, and see thee ill.

Gaunt. Now, he that made me knows I see thee ill;
Ill in myself to see, and in thee seeing ill.
Thy death-bed is no lesser than thy land 95
Wherein thou liest in reputation sick:
And thou, too careless patient as thou art,
Committ'st thy anointed body to the cure
Of those physicians that first wounded thee:
A thousand flatterers sit within thy crown, 100
Whose compass is no bigger than thy head;
And yet, incaged in so small a verge,
The waste is no whit lesser than thy land.
O! had thy grandsire, with a prophet's eye,
Seen how his son's son should destroy his sons, 105
From forth thy reach he would have laid thy shame,

83 **inherits**: owns. 84 **nicely**: with unnatural subtlety, fantastically. 85 **to mock itself**: by mocking at itself. 86–7 Since you treat our family and name mockingly by banishing my heir, I flatter you by imitating you. 88 **flatter with**: = flatter (hence Folio omits 'with'). 94 I am sick from inward causes, and so see badly, and also from seeing wickedness in you. 95 **no lesser than**: nothing less than. 102 **verge**: margin, edge, and so enclosing ring (or compass) of the crown. [*N*].

Deposing thee before thou wert possess'd,
Which art possess'd now to depose thyself.
Why, cousin, wert thou regent of the world,
It were a shame to let this land by lease; 110
But for thy world enjoying but this land,
Is it not more than shame to shame it so?
Landlord of England art thou now, not king:
Thy state of law is bond-slave to the law,
And—

K. Richard. And thou a lunatic lean-witted fool, 115
Presuming on an ague's privilege,
Dar'st with thy frozen admonition
Make pale our cheek, chasing the royal blood
With fury from his native residence.
Now, by my seat's right royal majesty, 120
Wert thou not brother to great Edward's son,—
This tongue that runs so roundly in thy head
Should run thy head from thy unreverent shoulders.

Gaunt. O! spare me not, my brother Edward's son,
For that I was his father Edward's son. 125
That blood already, like the pelican,
Hast thou tapp'd out and drunkenly carous'd:
My brother Gloucester, plain well-meaning soul,—
Whom fair befall in heaven 'mongst happy souls!—
May be a precedent and witness good 130
That thou respect'st not spilling Edward's blood:
Join with the present sickness that I have;
And thy unkindness be like crooked age,
To crop at once a too-long wither'd flower.

107 **possess'd**: in possession of the crown. 108 **possess'd**: as by an evil spirit. 114 **state of law**: legal status. 'As landlord, you must obey those laws, which, as king, you are above.' 117 **frozen admonition**: cold counsels of prudence. The *-ion* is two syllables. 122 **roundly**: outspokenly. 130 **precedent** in Eliz. Eng. usually = 'instance in proof' rather than 'example to follow'. 131 **respect'st not**: do not mind.

Live in thy shame, but die not shame with thee! 135
These words hereafter thy tormentors be!
Convey me to my bed, then to my grave:
Love they to live that love and honour have.
[*Exit, borne out by his* Attendants

K. Richard. And let them die that age and sullens have;
For both hast thou, and both become the grave. 140

York. I do beseech your majesty, impute his words
To wayward sickliness and age in him:
He loves you, on my life, and holds you dear
As Harry, Duke of Hereford, were he here.

K. Richard. Right, you say true: as Hereford's love, so his;
As theirs, so mine; and all be as it is. 146

Enter NORTHUMBERLAND.

Northumberland. My liege, old Gaunt commends him to your majesty.

K. Richard. What says he?

Northumberland. Nay, nothing; all is said:
His tongue is now a stringless instrument; 150
Words, life, and all, old Lancaster hath spent.

York. Be York the next that must be bankrupt so!
Though death be poor, it ends a mortal woe.

K. Richard. The ripest fruit first falls, and so doth he:
His time is spent; our pilgrimage must be. 155
So much for that. Now for our Irish wars.
We must supplant those rough rug-headed kerns,
Which live like venom where no venom else
But only they have privilege to live.

138 **Love they to live:** let them enjoy life. 139 **sullens:** sullen temper, sulks. 153 **death:** the state of being dead. 155 **our pilgrimage must be:** our turn to make our (death) journey is to come. Some interpret, 'We must go on with life, finish our (earthly) pilgrimage'. 157 **supplant:** oust (from power). **rug-headed:** with shaggy hair. [*N*]. **kerns:** light-armed Irish soldiers. 158 **venom:** reptiles. [*N*].

And for these great affairs do ask some charge, 160
Towards our assistance we do seize to us
The plate, coin, revenues, and moveables,
Whereof our uncle Gaunt did stand possess'd.
York. How long shall I be patient? Ah! how long
Shall tender duty make me suffer wrong? 165
Not Gloucester's death, nor Hereford's banishment,
Not Gaunt's rebukes, nor England's private wrongs,
Nor the prevention of poor Bolingbroke
About his marriage, nor my own disgrace,
Have ever made me sour my patient cheek, 170
Or bend one wrinkle on my sovereign's face.
I am the last of noble Edward's sons,
Of whom thy father, Prince of Wales, was first;
In war was never lion rag'd more fierce,
In peace was never gentle lamb more mild, 175
Than was that young and princely gentleman.
His face thou hast, for even so look'd he,
Accomplish'd with the number of thy hours;
But when he frown'd, it was against the French,
And not against his friends; his noble hand 180
Did win what he did spend, and spent not that
Which his triumphant father's hand had won:
His hands were guilty of no kindred's blood,
But bloody with the enemies of his kin.
O, Richard! York is too far gone with grief, 185
Or else he never would compare between.
K. Richard. Why, uncle, what's the matter?
York. O! my liege.
Pardon me, if you please; if not, I, pleas'd

160 **ask some charge**: involve expenditure. 165 **tender duty**: over-scrupulous loyalty to the king. 167 **Gaunt's rebukes**: Richard's rude behaviour to Gaunt. 177 **Accomplish'd with**: furnished with, i.e. at your age. 186 **between**: i.e. between you and your father. York breaks down.

Not to be pardon'd, am content withal.
Seek you to seize and gripe into your hands 190
The royalties and rights of banish'd Hereford?
Is not Gaunt dead, and doth not Hereford live?
Was not Gaunt just, and is not Harry true?
Did not the one deserve to have an heir?
Is not his heir a well-deserving son? 195
Take Hereford's rights away, and take from Time
His charters and his customary rights;
Let not to-morrow then ensue to-day;
Be not thyself; for how art thou a king
But by fair sequence and succession? 200
Now, afore God,—God forbid I say true!—
If you do wrongfully seize Hereford's rights,
Call in the letters-patent that he hath
By his attorneys-general to sue
His livery, and deny his offer'd homage, 205
You pluck a thousand dangers on your head,
You lose a thousand well-disposed hearts,
And prick my tender patience to those thoughts
Which honour and allegiance cannot think.

K. Richard. Think what you will: we seize into our hands
His plate, his goods, his money, and his lands. 211

York. I'll not be by the while: my liege, farewell:
What will ensue hereof, there's none can tell;

189 **withal:** with that, therewith. 191 **royalties:** rights, especially as a member of the royal house. 196–7 Time makes son succeed father, makes elder son have rights before younger; if you take Hereford's right of succession away, you deprive Time of this power. 198 **ensue:** follow upon (rarely used transitively). 199 **Be not thyself:** i.e. If you behave like this, you undermine your own position. 201 **God forbid I say true:** may my supposition not be realized. 203 **letters-patent:** letters by which some rights are conferred. [*N*]. 204 **attorneys-general:** those given power to act for him in all his affairs. 205 **livery:** delivery. [*N*]. **deny:** refuse. [*N*].

But by bad courses may be understood
That their events can never fall out good. [*Exit.*
K. Richard. Go, Bushy, to the Earl of Wiltshire straight:
Bid him repair to us to Ely House
To see this business. To-morrow next
We will for Ireland; and 'tis time, I trow:
And we create, in absence of ourself, 220
Our uncle York lord governor of England;
For he is just, and always lov'd us well.
Come on, our queen: to-morrow must we part;
Be merry, for our time of stay is short. [*Flourish.*

[*Exeunt* KING, QUEEN, BUSHY, AUMERLE, GREEN, *and* BAGOT.

Northumberland. Well, lords, the Duke of Lancaster is dead. 225
Ross. And living too; for now his son is duke.
Willoughby. Barely in title, not in revenue.
Northumberland. Richly in both, if justice had her right.
Ross. My heart is great; but it must break with silence,
Ere 't be disburden'd with a liberal tongue. 230
Northumberland. Nay, speak thy mind; and let him ne'er speak more
That speaks thy words again to do thee harm!
Willoughby. Tends that thou'dst speak to the Duke of Hereford?
If it be so, out with it boldly, man;
Quick is mine ear to hear of good towards him. 235
Ross. No good at all that I can do for him,
Unless you call it good to pity him,
Bereft and gelded of his patrimony.

214 **by:** with regard to. 215 **events:** issues. 218 **see:** see to. **business:** three syllables. **To-morrow next:** next morning. 229 **great:** full to overflowing. 230 **liberal:** too free, incautious. 233 **thou'dst:** thou wouldest. 238 **gelded of his patrimony:** having had his inheritance cut away.

Northumberland. Now, afore God, 'tis shame such wrongs are borne
In him, a royal prince, and many moe 240
Of noble blood in this declining land.
The king is not himself, but basely led
By flatterers; and what they will inform,
Merely in hate, 'gainst any of us all,
That will the king severely prosecute 245
'Gainst us, our lives, our children, and our heirs.
Ross. The commons hath he pill'd with grievous taxes,
And quite lost their hearts: the nobles hath he fin'd
For ancient quarrels, and quite lost their hearts.
Willoughby. And daily new exactions are devis'd; 250
As blanks, benevolences, and I wot not what:
But what, o' God's name, doth become of this?
Northumberland. Wars have not wasted it, for warr'd he hath not,
But basely yielded upon compromise
That which his ancestors achiev'd with blows. 255
More hath he spent in peace than they in wars.
Ross. The Earl of Wiltshire hath the realm in farm.
Willoughby. The king's grown bankrupt, like a broken man.
Northumberland. Reproach and dissolution hangeth over him.
Ross. He hath not money for these Irish wars, 260
His burdenous taxations notwithstanding,
But by the robbing of the banish'd duke.
North. His noble kinsman: most degenerate king!

239–40 **wrongs . . . in him**: wrongs done to him. **moe**: more. 243 **what . . . inform**: whatever they care to tell. 245 **prosecute**: punish. 247 **pill'd**: peeled, plundered (cf. 'pillage'). 251 **blanks**: see I. iv. 48. **benevolences**: forced loans (first exacted by Edward IV in 1473, as a token of goodwill to the throne). 254 **compromise**: agreement by concessions. 258 **broken**: a common Elizabethan word for 'bankrupt'.

But, lords, we hear this fearful tempest sing,
Yet seek no shelter to avoid the storm; 265
We see the wind sit sore upon our sails,
And yet we strike not, but securely perish.

Ross. We see the very wrack that we must suffer;
And unavoided is the danger now,
For suffering so the causes of our wrack. 270

North. Not so: even through the hollow eyes of death
I spy life peering; but I dare not say
How near the tidings of our comfort is.

Willoughby. Nay, let us share thy thoughts, as thou dost ours.

Ross. Be confident to speak, Northumberland: 275
We three are but thyself: and, speaking so,
Thy words are but as thoughts; therefore, be bold.

Northumberland. Then thus: I have from Port le Blanc, a bay
In Brittany, receiv'd intelligence
That Harry Duke of Hereford, Rainold Lord Cobham, 280
That late broke from the Duke of Exeter,
His brother, Archbishop late of Canterbury,
Sir Thomas Erpingham, Sir John Ramston,
Sir John Norbery, Sir Robert Waterton, and Francis Quoint,
All these well furnish'd by the Duke of Britaine, 285
With eight tall ships, three thousand men of war,
Are making hither with all due expedience,
And shortly mean to touch our northern shore.
Perhaps they had ere this, but that they stay

266 **sit:** used of a steady pressure or oppression, e.g. of guilt. 267 **strike:** lower our sails. **securely:** careless of danger (Latin *sine cura*). 269 **unavoided:** unavoidable, inevitable. 273 **tidings:** singular noun, cf. 'news'. 281 **late broke from:** i.e. escaped from his house. [*N*]. 286 **tall:** large, stout. **men of war:** soldiers. 287 **expedience:** speed, expedition; cf. I. iv. 39.

The first departing of the king for Ireland. 290
If then we shall shake off our slavish yoke,
Imp out our drooping country's broken wing,
Redeem from broking pawn the blemish'd crown,
Wipe off the dust that hides our sceptre's gilt,
And make high majesty look like itself, 295
Away with me in post to Ravenspurgh;
But if you faint, as fearing to do so,
Stay and be secret, and myself will go.

Ross. To horse, to horse! urge doubts to them that fear.

Willo. Hold out my horse, and I will first be there. 300

[*Exeunt.*

Scene II. The Same. A Room in the Palace

Enter QUEEN, BUSHY, *and* BAGOT.

Bushy. Madam, your majesty is too much sad:
You promis'd, when you parted with the king,
To lay aside life-harming heaviness,
And entertain a cheerful disposition.

Queen. To please the king I did; to please myself 5
I cannot do it; yet I know no cause
Why I should welcome such a guest as grief,
Save bidding farewell to so sweet a guest
As my sweet Richard: yet, again, methinks,
Some unborn sorrow, ripe in fortune's womb, 10
Is coming towards me, and my inward soul
With nothing trembles; at some thing it grieves

290 **The first departing:** till the king has first departed. 292 **Imp out:** repair, engraft new feathers on to (metaphor from falconry). 293 **Redeem . . . crown:** i.e. Richard has sold the use of his royal powers for money; we shall prevent any further abuse. In Eliz. Eng. a broker = a go-between, a pander. 300 **Hold out:** if he hold out, let him but hold out.

3 **life-harming:** every sigh or groan was supposed to cause the loss of a drop of blood. 12 **nothing:** the 'unborn sorrow' of l. 10.

More than with parting from my lord the king.
Bushy. Each substance of a grief hath twenty shadows,
Which show like grief itself, but are not so. 15
For sorrow's eye, glazed with blinding tears,
Divides one thing entire to many objects;
Like perspectives, which rightly gaz'd upon
Show nothing but confusion; ey'd awry
Distinguish form: so your sweet majesty, 20
Looking awry upon your lord's departure,
Finds shapes of grief more than himself to wail;
Which, look'd on as it is, is nought but shadows
Of what it is not. Then, thrice-gracious queen,
More than your lord's departure weep not: more 's not seen;
Or if it be, 'tis with false sorrow's eye, 26
Which for things true weeps things imaginary.
Queen. It may be so; but yet my inward soul
Persuades me it is otherwise: howe'er it be,
I cannot but be sad, so heavy sad, 30
As, though in thinking on no thought I think,
Makes me with heavy nothing faint and shrink.
Bushy. 'Tis nothing but conceit, my gracious lady.
Queen. 'Tis nothing less: conceit is still deriv'd
From some forefather grief; mine is not so, 35
For nothing hath begot my something grief;
Or something hath the nothing that I grieve:
'Tis in reversion that I do possess;

14 **substance of a grief**: substantial, real grief. **shadows**: appearances, deluding images. 16–17 i.e. Tears distort whatever is seen through them, make one thing appear many; so your grief multiplies your single cause of sorrow, the king's departure, into many. 18 **pérspectives**: a kind of mirror. [*N*]. 19 **awry**: crooked, sideways. [*N*]. 31 **though . . . think**: though I concentrate on thinking of nothing. 33 **conceit**: fancy, imagination. (III. ii. 166 shows how the sense of 'vanity' might be acquired.) 38 **reversion . . . possess**: to possess in reversion = to be heir to. [*N*]. **that**: which.

But what it is, that is not yet known; what
I cannot name; 'tis nameless woe, I wot. 40

Enter GREEN.

Green. God save your majesty! and well met, gentlemen:
I hope the king is not yet shipp'd for Ireland.
Queen. Why hop'st thou so? 'tis better hope he is,
For his designs crave haste, his haste good hope:
Then wherefore dost thou hope he is not shipp'd? 45
Green. That he, our hope, might have retir'd his power,
And driven into despair an enemy's hope,
Who strongly hath set footing in this land:
The banish'd Bolingbroke repeals himself,
And with uplifted arms is safe arriv'd 50
At Ravenspurgh.
Queen. Now God in heaven forbid!
Green. Ah! madam, 'tis too true: and that is worse,
The Lord Northumberland, his son young Henry Percy,
The Lords of Ross, Beaumond, and Willoughby,
With all their powerful friends, are fled to him. 55
Bushy. Why have you not proclaim'd Northumberland
And all the rest of the revolted faction traitors?
Green. We have: whereupon the Earl of Worcester
Hath broke his staff, resign'd his stewardship,
And all the household servants fled with him 60
To Bolingbroke.
Queen. So, Green, thou art the midwife to my woe,
And Bolingbroke my sorrow's dismal heir:
Now hath my soul brought forth her prodigy,
And I, a gasping new-deliver'd mother, 65

46 **retir'd**: brought back. **power**: forces (as frequently in Shakespeare). 49 **repeals**: recalls. 52 **that**: demonstrative, 'what, that which'. 63 **heir**: offspring, cf. ll. 10, 11. 64 **prodigy**: something which is a sign of evil to come; hence, a monstrous or unnatural birth. 65 **a gasping new deliver'd mother**: a mother exhausted from bearing her child.

Have woe to woe, sorrow to sorrow join'd.

Bushy. Despair not, madam.

Queen. Who shall hinder me?

I will despair, and be at enmity
With cozening hope: he is a flatterer,
A parasite, a keeper-back of death, 70
Who gently would dissolve the bands of life,
Which false hope lingers in extremity.

Enter YORK.

Green. Here comes the Duke of York.

Queen. With signs of war about his aged neck:
O! full of careful business are his looks. 75
Uncle, for God's sake, speak comfortable words.

York. Should I do so, I should belie my thoughts:
Comfort's in heaven, and we are on the earth,
Where nothing lives but crosses, cares, and grief.
Your husband, he is gone to save far off, 80
Whilst others come to make him lose at home:
Here am I left to underprop his land,
Who, weak with age, cannot support myself.
Now comes the sick hour that his surfeit made;
Now shall he try his friends that flatter'd him. 85

Enter a Servant.

Servant. My lord, your son was gone before I came.

York. He was? Why, so! go all which way it will!
The nobles they are fled, the commons they are cold,

66 **woe to woe**: i.e. my child, Bolingbroke's return, is only an additional grief instead of the joy that a new-born baby is to its mother. 69 **cozening**: deluding, deceiving. 71 **Who**: i.e. death. **dissolve**: unloose. 72 **Which**: i.e. life. **lingers**: makes to drag on. 74 **signs of war**: i.e. throat-piece or gorget of mail. 75 **careful**: anxious. 76 **Uncle**: scans as one syllable. 84 **surfeit**: see II. i. 37, &c. 87 **Why, so! go . . .**: well then, let what will come to pass; cf. II. i. 146.

And will, I fear, revolt on Hereford's side.
Sirrah, get thee to Plashy, to my sister Gloucester; 90
Bid her send me presently a thousand pound.
Hold, take my ring.
Servant. My lord, I had forgot to tell your lordship:
To-day, as I came by, I called there;
But I shall grieve you to report the rest. 95
York. What is't, knave?
Servant. An hour before I came the duchess died.
York. God for his mercy! what a tide of woes
Comes rushing on this woeful land at once!
I know not what to do: I would to God,— 100
So my untruth had not provok'd him to it,—
The king had cut off my head with my brother's.
What! are there no posts dispatch'd for Ireland?
How shall we do for money for these wars?
Come, sister,—cousin, I would say,—pray, pardon me.—
Go, fellow, get thee home; provide some carts 106
And bring away the armour that is there. [*Exit* Servant.
Gentlemen, will you go muster men? If I know
How or which way to order these affairs
Thus thrust disorderly into my hands, 110
Never believe me. Both are my kinsmen:
The one is my sovereign, whom both my oath
And duty bids defend; the other again
Is my kinsman, whom the king hath wrong'd,
Whom conscience and my kindred bids to right. 115
Well, somewhat we must do. Come, cousin,
I'll dispose of you. Gentlemen, go muster up your men,
And meet me presently at Berkeley Castle.
I should to Plashy too:
But time will not permit. All is uneven, 120

92 **take my ring:** i.e. to show that he really came from York.
98 **God:** (I) pray God. 101 **untruth:** disloyalty. Cf. 'true' in II. i. 193. 102 **brother's:** i.e. Gloucester's. [*N*].

And every thing is left at six and seven.
[*Exeunt* YORK *and* QUEEN.

Bushy. The wind sits fair for news to go to Ireland,
But none returns. For us to levy power
Proportionable to the enemy
Is all unpossible. 125

Green. Besides, our nearness to the king in love
Is near the hate of those love not the king.

Bagot. And that's the wavering commons; for their love
Lies in their purses, and whoso empties them,
By so much fills their hearts with deadly hate. 130

Bushy. Wherein the king stands generally condemn'd.

Bagot. If judgment lie in them, then so do we,
Because we ever have been near the king.

Green. Well, I'll for refuge straight to Bristol Castle;
The Earl of Wiltshire is already there. 135

Bushy. Thither will I with you; for little office
Will the hateful commons perform for us,
Except like curs to tear us all to pieces.
Will you go along with us?

Bagot. No; I will to Ireland to his majesty. 140
Farewell: if heart's presages be not vain,
We three here part that ne'er shall meet again.

Bushy. That's as York thrives to beat back Bolingbroke.

Green. Alas, poor duke! the task he undertakes
Is numbering sands and drinking oceans dry: 145
Where one on his side fights, thousands will fly.
Farewell at once; for once, for all, and ever.

Bushy. Well, we may meet again.

Bagot. I fear me, never. [*Exeunt.*

127 Makes us subject to the hatred of those who do not like the king. 132 If they can pass judgement on the king, they will do so on us, too. 137 **hateful**: probably 'full of hate' rather than 'detestable'. 143 That depends on whether York succeeds in beating back Bolingbroke.

Scene III. THE WOLDS IN GLOUCESTERSHIRE

Enter BOLINGBROKE *and* NORTHUMBERLAND, *with Forces.*

Bolingbroke. How far is it, my lord, to Berkeley now?
Northumberland. Believe me, noble lord,
I am a stranger here in Gloucestershire:
These high wild hills and rough uneven ways
Draw out our miles and make them wearisome; 5
But yet your fair discourse hath been as sugar,
Making the hard way sweet and delectable.
But I bethink me what a weary way
From Ravenspurgh to Cotswold will be found
In Ross and Willoughby, wanting your company, 10
Which, I protest, hath very much beguil'd
The tediousness and process of my travel:
But theirs is sweeten'd with the hope to have
The present benefit which I possess;
And hope to joy is little less in joy 15
Than hope enjoy'd: by this the weary lords
Shall make their way seem short, as mine hath done
By sight of what I have, your noble company.
Bolingbroke. Of much less value is my company
Than your good words. But who comes here? 20

Enter HENRY PERCY.

Northumberland. It is my son, young Harry Percy,
Sent from my brother Worcester, whencesoever.
Harry, how fares your uncle?
H. Percy. I had thought, my lord, to have learn'd his health of you.

12 **tediousness and process:** long and weary course. 15
Anticipation is almost equal to realization. 'Hope' first = the feeling, then = the thing hoped for.

Northumberland. Why, is he not with the queen? 25

H. Percy. No, my good lord; he hath forsook the court,
Broken his staff of office, and dispers'd
The household of the king.

Northumberland. What was his reason?
He was not so resolv'd when last we spake together.

H. Percy. Because your lordship was proclaimed traitor.
But he, my lord, is gone to Ravenspurgh, 31
To offer service to the Duke of Hereford,
And sent me over by Berkeley to discover
What power the Duke of York had levied there;
Then with direction to repair to Ravenspurgh. 35

North. Have you forgot the Duke of Hereford, boy?

H. Percy. No, my good lord; for that is not forgot
Which ne'er I did remember: to my knowledge
I never in my life did look on him.

Northumberland. Then learn to know him now: this is the duke. 40

H. Percy. My gracious lord, I tender you my service,
Such as it is, being tender, raw, and young,
Which elder days shall ripen and confirm
To more approved service and desert.

Bolingbroke. I thank thee, gentle Percy; and be sure 45
I count myself in nothing else so happy
As in a soul remembering my good friends;
And as my fortune ripens with thy love,
It shall be still thy true love's recompense:
My heart this covenant makes, my hand thus seals it. 50

North. How far is it to Berkeley? and what stir
Keeps good old York there with his men of war?

47 **As in a soul remembering:** as in having a heart which remembers. 48 **ripens with:** either (1) with the help of, through, or (2) simultaneously with. 52 **Keeps:** York is the subject.

H. Percy. There stands the castle, by yon tuft of trees,
Mann'd with three hundred men, as I have heard;
And in it are the Lords of York, Berkeley, and Seymour;
None else of name and noble estimate. 56

Enter ROSS *and* WILLOUGHBY

North. Here come the Lords of Ross and Willoughby,
Bloody with spurring, fiery-red with haste.
Bolingbroke. Welcome, my lords. I wot your love pursues
A banish'd traitor; all my treasury 60
Is yet but unfelt thanks, which, more enrich'd,
Shall be your love and labour's recompense.
Ross. Your presence makes us rich, most noble lord.
Willoughby. And far surmounts our labour to attain it.
Bolingbroke. Evermore thanks, the exchequer of the poor;
Which, till my infant fortune comes to years, 66
Stands for my bounty. But who comes here?

Enter BERKELEY.

Northumberland. It is my Lord of Berkeley, as I guess.
Berkeley. My Lord of Hereford, my message is to you.
Bolingbroke. My lord, my answer is—to Lancaster; 70
And I am come to seek that name in England;
And I must find that title in your tongue
Before I make reply to aught you say.
Berkeley. Mistake me not, my lord; 'tis not my meaning
To raze one title of your honour out: 75
To you, my lord, I come, what lord you will,
From the most gracious regent of this land,
The Duke of York, to know what pricks you on

59 **wot**: know. 61 **unfelt**: i.e. by the recipients. He hopes to be able soon to give substantial favours. **which, more enrich'd**: i.e. when 'thanks' have gifts or favours added to them. 65 **exchequer**: treasury. 75 **raze**: cut down. **title**: there is probably a play on 'tittle'.

To take advantage of the absent time
And fright our native peace with self-born arms. 80

Enter YORK, *attended.*

Bolingbroke. I shall not need transport my words by you:
Here comes his Grace in person.
My noble uncle! [*Kneels.*

York. Show me thy humble heart, and not thy knee,
Whose duty is deceivable and false.

Bolingbroke. My gracious uncle— 85

York. Tut, tut!
Grace me no grace, nor uncle me no uncle:
I am no traitor's uncle; and that word 'grace
In an ungracious mouth is but profane.
Why have those banish'd and forbidden legs 90
Dar'd once to touch a dust of England's ground
But then, more 'why?', why have they dar'd to march
So many miles upon her peaceful bosom,
Frighting her pale-fac'd villages with war
And ostentation of despised arms? 95
Com'st thou because the anointed king is hence?
Why, foolish boy, the king is left behind,
And in my loyal bosom lies his power.
Were I but now the lord of such hot youth
As when brave Gaunt thy father, and myself, 100
Rescu'd the Black Prince, that young Mars of men,
From forth the ranks of many thousand French.
O! then, how quickly should this arm of mine,
Now prisoner to the palsy, chastise thee

79 **absent time**: time when the king is absent. 84 **duty**: respectful behaviour. **deceivable**: capable of deceiving. 91 **a dust**: a particle of dust. 92 **more 'why?'**: there are other questions which require an answer. 95 **despised**: contemptible, cf. 'detested', l. 109, and 'unavoided', II. i. 269. 96 **hence**: absent. 104 **palsy**: paralysis: used generally of senile debility. **chastise**: chástise.

And minister correction to thy fault! 105

Bolingbroke. My gracious uncle, let me know my fault:
On what condition stands it, and wherein?

York. Even in condition of the worst degree,
In gross rebellion and detested treason:
Thou art a banish'd man, and here art come 110
Before the expiration of thy time,
In braving arms against thy sovereign.

Bolingbroke. As I was banish'd, I was banish'd Hereford:
But as I come, I come for Lancaster.
And, noble uncle, I beseech your Grace 115
Look on my wrongs with an indifferent eye:
You are my father, for methinks in you
I see old Gaunt alive: O! then, my father,
Will you permit that I shall stand condemn'd
A wandering vagabond; my rights and royalties 120
Pluck'd from my arms perforce and given away
To upstart unthrifts? Wherefore was I born?
If that my cousin king be King of England,
It must be granted I am Duke of Lancaster.
You have a son, Aumerle, my noble kinsman; 125
Had you first died, and he been thus trod down,
He should have found his uncle Gaunt a father,
To rouse his wrongs and chase them to the bay.
I am denied to sue my livery here,
And yet my letters-patent give me leave: 130
My father's goods are all distrain'd and sold,

107 **On what . . . wherein?**: on what quality or condition of mind does it depend, shown in what actions? [*N*]. 112 **braving**: defiant. 114 **for Lancaster**: in the character (or person) of Lancaster. 116 **indifferent**: impartial. 120 **royalties**: see II. i. 191. 122 **unthrifts**: spendthrifts, profligates (like the king's favourites). 128 **rouse**: start in flight. **his wrongs**: the metaphor requires rather 'his wrongers'. **to the bay**: to the end, where the animal turns on the dogs. 129–30 See II. i. 202–4 and notes. 131 **distrain'd**: confiscated.

And these and all are all amiss employ'd.
What would you have me do? I am a subject,
And challenge law: attorneys are denied me,
And therefore personally I lay my claim 135
To my inheritance of free descent.

North. The noble duke hath been too much abus'd.

Ross. It stands your Grace upon to do him right.

Willo. Base men by his endowments are made great.

York. My lords of England, let me tell you this: 140
I have had feeling of my cousin's wrongs,
And labour'd all I could to do him right;
But in this kind to come, in braving arms,
Be his own carver and cut out his way,
To find out right with wrong, it may not be; 145
And you that do abet him in this kind
Cherish rebellion and are rebels all.

North. The noble duke hath sworn his coming is
But for his own; and for the right of that
We all have strongly sworn to give him aid; 150
And let him ne'er see joy that breaks that oath!

York. Well, well, I see the issue of these arms:
I cannot mend it, I must needs confess,
Because my power is weak and all ill left;
But if I could, by him that gave me life, 155
I would attach you all and make you stoop
Unto the sovereign mercy of the king;
But since I cannot, be it known to you
I do remain as neuter. So, fare you well;
Unless you please to enter in the castle 160

134 **challenge law**: claim my rights according to law. **attorneys**: cf. II. i. 204. 138 **It stands . . . upon**: it is your Grace's duty. 139 **by his endowments**: out of Bolingbroke's properties; cf. III. i. 22–3. 143 **kind**: manner, fashion. 154 **ill left**: probably = left in disorder (cf. II. ii. 121); possibly = badly provided for. 156 **attach**: arrest. 159 **neuter**: neutral.

And there repose you for this night.
Bolingbroke. An offer, uncle, that we will accept:
But we must win your Grace to go with us
To Bristol Castle; which they say is held
By Bushy, Bagot, and their complices, 165
The caterpillars of the commonwealth,
Which I have sworn to weed and pluck away.
York. It may be I will go with you; but yet I'll pause;
For I am loath to break our country's laws.
Nor friends nor foes, to me welcome you are: 170
Things past redress are now with me past care. [*Exeunt.*

Scene IV. A Camp in Wales

Enter SALISBURY *and a* Captain.

Captain. My Lord of Salisbury, we have stay'd ten days,
And hardly kept our countrymen together,
And yet we hear no tidings from the king;
Therefore we will disperse ourselves: farewell.
Salisbury. Stay yet another day, thou trusty Welshman:
The king reposeth all his confidence in thee. 6
Captain. 'Tis thought the king is dead: we will not stay.
The bay-trees in our country are all wither'd
And meteors fright the fixed stars of heaven,
The pale-fac'd moon looks bloody on the earth 10
And lean-look'd prophets whisper fearful change,
Rich men look sad and ruffians dance and leap,
The one in fear to lose what they enjoy,
The other to enjoy by rage and war:
These signs forerun the death or fall of kings. 15
Farewell: our countrymen are gone and fled,
As well assur'd Richard their king is dead. [*Exit.*

165 **complices:** accomplices. 166 **caterpillars:** a popular Eliz. word for 'parasites', 'unproductive people'.

10 **looks bloody on:** turns a bloody aspect towards. 11 **lean-look'd:** lean-looking. 14 **to enjoy:** in hope to enjoy.

Salisbury. Ah, Richard! with the eyes of heavy mind
I see thy glory like a shooting star
Fall to the base earth from the firmament. 20
Thy sun sets weeping in the lowly west,
Witnessing storms to come, woe, and unrest,
Thy friends are fled to wait upon thy foes,
And crossly to thy good all fortune goes. [*Exit.*

18 **heavy mind:** anxiety, forethought. 22 **Witnessing:** indicating, foretelling. 24 **crossly:** adversely.

ACT III

Scene I. BRISTOL. BOLINGBROKE'S CAMP

Enter BOLINGBROKE, YORK, NORTHUMBERLAND, HENRY PERCY, WILLOUGHBY, ROSS; Officers *behind, with* BUSHY *and* GREEN *prisoners.*

Bolingbroke. Bring forth these men.
Bushy and Green, I will not vex your souls—
Since presently your souls must part your bodies—
With too much urging your pernicious lives,
For 'twere no charity; yet, to wash your blood 5
From off my hands, here in the view of men
I will unfold some causes of your deaths.
You have misled a prince, a royal king,
A happy gentleman in blood and lineaments,
By you unhappied and disfigur'd clean: 10
You have in manner with your sinful hours
Made a divorce betwixt his queen and him,
Broke the possession of a royal bed,
And stain'd the beauty of a fair queen's cheeks
With tears drawn from her eyes by your foul wrongs. 15
Myself, a prince by fortune of my birth,
Near to the king in blood, and near in love
Till you did make him misinterpret me,
Have stoop'd my neck under your injuries,
And sigh'd my English breath in foreign clouds 20
Eating the bitter bread of banishment;
Whilst you have fed upon my signories,

3 **part**: leave. [*N*]. 4 **urging**: calling attention to. 9 **A happy . . . lineaments**: a gentleman fortunate in birth and personal appearance. 10 **unhappied**: cf. 'undeaf', II. i. 16. **clean**: entirely. 11 **in manner**: in a way, after a fashion. 22 **signories**: lands over which he was 'seigneur' or lord.

Dispark'd my parks, and felled my forest woods,
From mine own windows torn my household coat,
Raz'd out my impress, leaving me no sign, 25
Save men's opinions and my living blood,
To show the world I am a gentleman.
This and much more, much more than twice all this,
Condemns you to the death. See them deliver'd over
To execution and the hand of death. 30

Bushy. More welcome is the stroke of death to me
Than Bolingbroke to England. Lords, farewell.

Green. My comfort is, that heaven will take our souls
And plague injustice with the pains of hell.

Boling. My Lord Northumberland, see them dispatch'd.
[*Exeunt* NORTHUMBERLAND *and Others, with* BUSHY *and* GREEN.
Uncle, you say the queen is at your house; 36
For God's sake, fairly let her be entreated:
Tell her I send to her my kind commends;
Take special care my greetings be deliver'd.

York. A gentleman of mine I have dispatch'd 40
With letters of your love to her at large.

Bolingbroke. Thanks, gentle uncle. Come, lords, away
To fight with Glendower and his complices:
Awhile to work, and after holiday. [*Exeunt.*

23 **Dispark'd:** taken away the enclosures, i.e. converted parks into commons. 24 **household coat:** family coat of arms, which was often blazoned on the windows of great houses. 25 **impress:** crest or device adopted, frequently with a motto, in addition to the coat of arms. [*N*]. 37 **entreated:** treated. 38 **commends:** compliments. 41 **at large:** in full.

Scene II. THE COAST OF WALES. A CASTLE IN VIEW

Flourish: drums and trumpets. Enter KING RICHARD, *the* BISHOP OF CARLISLE, AUMERLE, *and* Soldiers.

K. Richard. Barkloughly Castle call they this at hand?
Aumerle. Yea, my lord. How brooks your Grace the air,
After your late tossing on the breaking seas?
K. Richard. Needs must I like it well: I weep for joy
To stand upon my kingdom once again. 5
Dear earth, I do salute thee with my hand,
Though rebels wound thee with their horses' hoofs:
As a long-parted mother with her child
Plays fondly with her tears and smiles in meeting,
So, weeping, smiling, greet I thee, my earth, 10
And do thee favour with my royal hands.
Feed not thy sovereign's foe, my gentle earth,
Nor with thy sweets comfort his ravenous sense;
But let thy spiders, that suck up thy venom,
And heavy-gaited toads lie in their way, 15
Doing annoyance to the treacherous feet
Which with usurping steps do trample thee.
Yield stinging nettles to mine enemies;
And when they from thy bosom pluck a flower,
Guard it, I pray thee, with a lurking adder 20
Whose double tongue may with a mortal touch
Throw death upon thy sovereign's enemies.
Mock not my senseless conjuration, lords:
This earth shall have a feeling and these stones
Prove armed soldiers, ere her native king 25

2 **brooks**: enjoys (usually 'endures, suffers'). 8 As a mother parted a long time *from* her child. 13 **ravenous sense**: greedy appetite. 15 **heavy-gaited**: of slow motion. 21 **double**: forked. **mortal**: deadly. 23 **senseless conjuration**: appeal to something which has no senses, and so 'unfelt', 'unheard' (*not* 'foolish').

Shall falter under foul rebellion's arms.

Carlisle. Fear not, my lord: that power that made you king
Hath power to keep you king in spite of all.
The means that heaven yields must be embrac'd,
And not neglected; else, if heaven would, 30
And we will not, heaven's offer we refuse,
The proffer'd means of succour and redress.

Aumerle. He means, my lord, that we are too remiss;
Whilst Bolingbroke, through our security,
Grows strong and great in substance and in friends. 35

K. Richard. Discomfortable cousin! know'st thou not
That when the searching eye of heaven is hid
Behind the globe, and lights the lower world,
Then thieves and robbers range abroad unseen,
In murders and in outrage bloody here; 40
But when, from under this terrestrial ball
He fires the proud tops of the eastern pines
And darts his light through every guilty hole,
Then murders, treasons, and detested sins,
The cloak of night being pluck'd from off their backs, 45
Stand bare and naked, trembling at themselves?
So when this thief, this traitor, Bolingbroke,
Who all this while hath revell'd in the night
Whilst we were wandering with the antipodes,
Shall see us rising in our throne, the east, 50
His treasons will sit blushing in his face,
Not able to endure the sight of day,
But self-affrighted tremble at his sin.
Not all the water in the rough rude sea
Can wash the balm from an anointed king; 55

34 **security**: careless over-confidence; cf. II. i. 267. 36 **Discomfortable**: discouraging; cf. II. ii. 76. 49 **antipodes**: properly, those whose feet are set against ours, on the opposite side of the globe.

The breath of worldly men cannot depose
The deputy elected by the Lord.
For every man that Bolingbroke hath press'd
To lift shrewd steel against our golden crown,
God for his Richard hath in heavenly pay 60
A glorious angel: then, if angels fight,
Weak men must fall, for heaven still guards the right.

Enter SALISBURY.

Welcome, my lord: how far off lies your power?
Salisbury. Nor near nor further off, my gracious lord,
Than this weak arm: discomfort guides my tongue 65
And bids me speak of nothing but despair.
One day too late, I fear me, noble lord,
Hath clouded all thy happy days on earth.
O! call back yesterday, bid time return,
And thou shalt have twelve thousand fighting men: 70
To-day, to-day, unhappy day too late,
O'erthrows thy joys, friends, fortune, and thy state;
For all the Welshmen, hearing thou wert dead,
Are gone to Bolingbroke, dispers'd, and fled.
Aumerle. Comfort, my liege! why looks your Grace so pale? 75
K. Richard. But now, the blood of twenty thousand men
Did triumph in my face, and they are fled;
And till so much blood thither come again
Have I not reason to look pale and dead?
All souls that will be safe, fly from my side; 80
For time hath set a blot upon my pride.
Aumerle. Comfort, my liege! remember who you are.
K. Richard. I had forgot myself. Am I not king?

58 **press'd**: forced into service 59 **shrewd**: used of material things = sharp; applied generally = biting, keen. 62 **still**: always. 64 **near**: nearer (probably due to slurred pronunciation). 76 **But now**: a moment ago.

Awake, thou sluggard majesty! thou sleepest.
Is not the king's name twenty thousand names? 85
Arm, arm, my name! a puny subject strikes
At thy great glory. Look not to the ground,
Ye favourites of a king: are we not high?
High be our thoughts: I know my uncle York
Hath power enough to serve our turn. But who comes
here? 90

Enter SIR STEPHEN SCROOP.

Scroop. More health and happiness betide my liege
Than can my care-tun'd tongue deliver him!

K. Richard. Mine ear is open and my heart prepar'd:
The worst is worldly loss thou canst unfold.
Say, is my kingdom lost? why, 'twas my care; 95
And what loss is it to be rid of care?
Strives Bolingbroke to be as great as we?
Greater he shall not be: if he serve God
We'll serve him too, and be his fellow so:
Revolt our subjects? that we cannot mend; 100
They break their faith to God as well as us:
Cry woe, destruction, ruin, loss, decay;
The worst is death, and death will have his day.

Scroop. Glad am I that your highness is so arm'd
To bear the tidings of calamity. 105
Like an unseasonable stormy day
Which makes the silver rivers drown their shores,
As if the world were all dissolv'd to tears,
So high above his limits swells the rage
Of Bolingbroke, covering your fearful land 110

91 **betide:** befall, happen to. 92 **care-tun'd:** tuned by care, i.e. prepared only for giving bad news. 95 **care:** (source of) anxiety. 99 **fellow:** equal. 102 **Cry woe:** announce (as by public proclamation). 103 **Death . . . day:** death must come some time anyhow.

With hard bright steel and hearts harder than steel.
White-beards have arm'd their thin and hairless scalps
Against thy majesty; and boys, with women's voices,
Strive to speak big, and clap their female joints
In stiff unwieldy arms against thy crown; 115
Thy very beadsmen learn to bend their bows
Of double-fatal yew against thy state;
Yea, distaff-women manage rusty bills
Against thy seat: both young and old rebel,
And all goes worse than I have power to tell. 120

K. Richard. Too well, too well thou tell'st a tale so ill.
Where is the Earl of Wiltshire? where is Bagot?
What is become of Bushy? where is Green?
That they have let the dangerous enemy
Measure our confines with such peaceful steps? 125
If we prevail, their heads shall pay for it.
I warrant they have made peace with Bolingbroke.

Scroop. Peace have they made with him, indeed, my lord.

K. Rich. O villains, vipers, damn'd without redemption!
Dogs, easily won to fawn on any man! 130
Snakes, in my heart-blood warm'd, that sting my heart!
Three Judases, each one thrice worse than Judas!
Would they make peace? terrible hell make war
Upon their spotted souls for this offence!

Scroop. Sweet love, I see, changing his property, 135
Turns to the sourest and most deadly hate.

112 **thin and hairless**: i.e. thin-haired and hairless. 114 **clap**: enclose. **female**: weak, not suited to bear armour. [*N*]. 116 **beadsmen**: pensioners who 'told their beads', i.e. prayed for those on whom they were dependent. 117 **double-fatal**: doubly fatal, since the leaves were poisonous and the wood was used for bows. 118 **distaff-women**: spinners. **bills**: a long-shafted weapon, the head of which ended as a spear, with an axe-blade on one side and a spike on the other. 119 **seat**: throne. 125 Cross the country unopposed. 134 **spotted**: with sin. 135 **his**: its. **property**: proper or distinctive quality.

Again uncurse their souls; their peace is made
With heads and not with hands: those whom you curse
Have felt the worst of death's destroying wound
And lie full low, grav'd in the hollow ground. 140

Aum. Is Bushy, Green, and the Earl of Wiltshire dead?

Scroop. Yea, all of them at Bristol lost their heads.

Aumerle. Where is the duke my father with his power?

K. Richard. No matter where. Of comfort no man speak:
Let's talk of graves, of worms, and epitaphs; 145
Make dust our paper, and with rainy eyes
Write sorrow on the bosom of the earth;
Let's choose executors and talk of wills:
And yet not so—for what can we bequeath
Save our deposed bodies to the ground? 150
Our lands, our lives, and all are Bolingbroke's,
And nothing can we call our own but death,
And that small model of the barren earth
Which serves as paste and cover to our bones.
For God's sake, let us sit upon the ground 155
And tell sad stories of the death of kings:
How some have been depos'd, some slain in war,
Some haunted by the ghosts they have depos'd,
Some poison'd by their wives, some sleeping kill'd;
All murder'd: for within the hollow crown 160
That rounds the mortal temples of a king
Keeps Death his court, and there the antick sits,
Scoffing his state and grinning at his pomp;
Allowing him a breath, a little scene,
To monarchize, be fear'd, and kill with looks, 165
Infusing him with self and vain conceit,

140 **grav'd**: buried. 158 **ghosts they**: ghosts of those whom. 161 **rounds**: surrounds. 162 **antick**: jester, clown. 163 **Scoffing**: scoffing at. 165 **monarchize**: play the king. 166 **Infusing**: filling. **self and vain conceit**: vain self-conceit. [*N*].

As if this flesh which walls about our life
Were brass impregnable; and humour'd thus
Comes at the last, and with a little pin
Bores through his castle wall, and farewell king! 170
Cover your heads, and mock not flesh and blood
With solemn reverence: throw away respect,
Tradition, form, and ceremonious duty,
For you have but mistook me all this while:
I live with bread like you, feel want, 175
Taste grief, need friends: subjected thus,
How can you say to me I am a king?

Carlisle. My lord, wise men ne'er sit and wail their woes,
But presently prevent the ways to wail.
To fear the foe, since fear oppresseth strength, 180
Gives in your weakness strength unto your foe,
And so your follies fight against yourself.
Fear and be slain; no worse can come to fight:
And fight and die is death destroying death;
Where fearing dying pays death servile breath. 185

Aumerle. My father hath a power, inquire of him
And learn to make a body of a limb.

K. Richard. Thou chid'st me well. Proud Bolingbroke, I come
To change blows with thee for our day of doom.
This ague-fit of fear is over-blown; 190
An easy task it is, to win our own.—
Say, Scroop, where lies our uncle with his power?
Speak sweetly, man, although thy looks be sour.

Scroop. Men judge by the complexion of the sky

168 **humour'd**: when the king had been humoured thus. [*N*]. 176 **subjected**: made subject to such needs (with a play on the word). 179 **presently**: at once (as nearly always). **prevent**: forestall (the causes of the grief). 180 **oppresseth**: destroys. 183 **to fight**: by fighting. [*N*]. 185 **Where**: whereas. 186 **a power**: troops. 187 Contrive to use his force as though it were a large army. 189 **change**: exchange.

The state and inclination of the day; 195
So may you by my dull and heavy eye,
My tongue hath but a heavier tale to say.
I play the torturer, by small and small
To lengthen out the worst that must be spoken.
Your uncle York is join'd with Bolingbroke, 200
And all your northern castles yielded up,
And all your southern gentlemen in arms
Upon his party.

K. Richard. Thou hast said enough.
[*To* AUMERLE.] Beshrew thee, cousin, which didst lead me forth
Of that sweet way I was in to despair! 205
What say you now? What comfort have we now?
By heaven, I'll hate him everlastingly
That bids me be of comfort any more.
Go to Flint Castle: there I'll pine away;
A king, woe's slave, shall kingly woe obey. 210
That power I have, discharge; and let them go
To ear the land that hath some hope to grow,
For I have none: let no man speak again
To alter this, for counsel is but vain.

Aumerle. My liege, one word.

K. Richard. He does me double wrong, 215
That wounds me with the flatteries of his tongue.
Discharge my followers: let them hence away,
From Richard's night to Bolingbroke's fair day. [*Exeunt.*

198 **by small and small**: little by little. 203 **party**: side; cf. III. iii. 115. The Folios read 'faction'. 204 **Beshrew thee**: curse thee. For Richard's change, cf. l. 36. 212 **ear**: till, plough. 'Let them give service where there is hope of reward.'

Scene III. WALES. BEFORE FLINT CASTLE

Enter, with drum and colours, BOLINGBROKE *and Forces;* YORK, NORTHUMBERLAND, *and Others.*

Bolingbroke. So that by this intelligence we learn
The Welshmen are dispers'd and Salisbury
Is gone to meet the king, who lately landed
With some few private friends upon this coast.
North. The news is very fair and good, my lord: 5
Richard not far from hence hath hid his head.
York. It would beseem the Lord Northumberland
To say, 'King Richard:' alack the heavy day
When such a sacred king should hide his head!
North. Your Grace mistakes; only to be brief 10
Left I his title out.
York. The time hath been,
Would you have been so brief with him, he would
Have been so brief with you, to shorten you,
For taking so the head, your whole head's length.
Boling. Mistake not, uncle, further than you should. 15
York. Take not, good cousin, further than you should,
Lest you mistake the heavens are o'er our heads.
Bolingbroke. I know it, uncle; and oppose not myself
Against their will. But who comes here?

Enter HENRY PERCY.

Welcome, Harry: what, will not this castle yield? 20
H. Percy. The castle royally is mann'd, my lord,
Against thy entrance.

13 **to shorten:** as to shorten. [*N*]. 15 **Mistake:** misinterpret. 16 **Take:** assume (power). 17 **mistake:** fail to recognize, forget.

Bolingbroke. Royally!
Why, it contains no king?
H. Percy. Yes, my good lord,
It doth contain a king: King Richard lies 25
Within the limits of yon lime and stone;
And with him are the Lord Aumerle, Lord Salisbury,
Sir Stephen Scroop; besides a clergyman
Of holy reverence; who, I cannot learn.
Northumberland. O! belike it is the Bishop of Carlisle.
Bolingbroke. [*To* NORTHUMBERLAND.] Noble lord, 31
Go to the rude ribs of that ancient castle,
Through brazen trumpet send the breath of parley
Into his ruin'd ears, and thus deliver:
Henry Bolingbroke 35
On both his knees doth kiss King Richard's hand,
And sends allegiance and true faith of heart
To his most royal person; hither come
Even at his feet to lay my arms and power,
Provided that my banishment repeal'd, 40
And lands restor'd again be freely granted.
If not, I'll use the advantage of my power,
And lay the summer's dust with showers of blood
Rain'd from the wounds of slaughter'd Englishmen:
The which, how far off from the mind of Bolingbroke 45
It is, such crimson tempest should bedrench
The fresh green lap of fair King Richard's land,
My stooping duty tenderly shall show.
Go, signify as much, while here we march
Upon the grassy carpet of this plain. 50
Let's march without the noise of threat'ning drum,

30 **belike**: very likely. 34 **his**: its, i.e. the castle's. **ears**: probably loopholes for defence. 40–1 Provided that the repeal of my banishment and the restoration of my lands be granted unconditionally. 46 **such**: that such. 48 **stooping duty**: loyalty expressed by bent knees (l. 36).

That from the castle's tatter'd battlements
Our fair appointments may be well perus'd.
Methinks King Richard and myself should meet
With no less terror than the elements 55
Of fire and water, when their thundering shock
At meeting tears the cloudy cheeks of heaven.
Be he the fire, I'll be the yielding water:
The rage be his, while on the earth I rain
My waters; on the earth, and not on him. 60
March on, and mark King Richard how he looks.

A Parley sounded, and answered by a Trumpet within. Flourish. Enter on the Walls KING RICHARD, *the* BISHOP OF CARLISLE, AUMERLE, SCROOP, *and* SALISBURY.

H. Percy. See, see, King Richard doth himself appear,
As doth the blushing discontented sun
From out the fiery portal of the east,
When he perceives the envious clouds are bent 65
To dim his glory and to stain the track
Of his bright passage to the occident.
York. Yet looks he like a king: behold, his eye,
As bright as is the eagle's, lightens forth
Controlling majesty: alack, alack, for woe, 70
That any harm should stain so fair a show!
K. Richard. [*To* NORTHUMBERLAND.] We are amaz'd; and thus long have we stood
To watch the fearful bending of thy knee,
Because we thought ourself thy lawful king:
And if we be, how dare thy joints forget 75
To pay their awful duty to our presence?

52 **tatter'd:** crenellated, indented. 67 **occident:** west.
69–70 **lightens . . . majesty:** expresses kingly power to dominate.
73 **To watch:** waiting for. **fearful:** full of fear (cf. III. ii. 110), as 'awful' (l. 76) = 'full of awe'.

If we be not, show us the hand of God
That hath dismiss'd us from our stewardship;
For well we know, no hand of blood and bone
Can gripe the sacred handle of our sceptre, 80
Unless he do profane, steal, or usurp.
And though you think that all, as you have done,
Have torn their souls by turning them from us,
And we are barren and bereft of friends;
Yet know, my master, God omnipotent, 85
Is mustering in his clouds on our behalf
Armies of pestilence; and they shall strike
Your children yet unborn and unbegot,
That lift your vassal hands against my head
And threat the glory of my precious crown. 90
Tell Bolingbroke,—for yond methinks he is,—
That every stride he makes upon my land
Is dangerous treason: he is come to open
The purple testament of bleeding war;
But ere the crown he looks for live in peace, 95
Ten thousand bloody crowns of mother's sons
Shall ill become the flower of England's face,
Change the complexion of her maid-pale peace
To scarlet indignation, and bedew
Her pastures' grass with faithful English blood. 100

North. The king of heaven forbid our lord the king
Should so with civil and uncivil arms
Be rush'd upon! Thy thrice-noble cousin,
Harry Bolingbroke, doth humbly kiss thy hand;

81 **profane:** commit sacrilege. 83 **torn their souls:** rent their allegiance and so perjured themselves—with a pun on 'turn'. 88–9 **Your children . . . That:** the children of you . . . that. 94 **purple:** blood-stained. **testament:** will (which must be opened before it can be carried out). [*N*]. 96 **crowns:** heads (with a pun on l. 95). 97 **ill become:** disfigure. **flower . . . face:** beauty of England. 102 **civil:** as of fellow-country-men. **uncivil:** rough, brutal.

And by the honourable tomb he swears, 105
That stands upon your royal grandsire's bones,
And by the royalties of both your bloods,
Currents that spring from one most gracious head,
And by the buried hand of war-like Gaunt,
And by the worth and honour of himself, 110
Comprising all that may be sworn or said,
His coming hither hath no further scope
Than for his lineal royalties and to beg
Enfranchisement immediate on his knees:
Which on thy royal party granted once, 115
His glittering arms he will commend to rust,
His barbed steeds to stables, and his heart
To faithful service of your majesty.
This swears he, as he is a prince, is just;
And, as I am a gentleman, I credit him. 120

K. Richard. Northumberland, say, thus the king returns:
His noble cousin is right welcome hither;
And all the number of his fair demands
Shall be accomplish'd without contradiction:
With all the gracious utterance thou hast 125
Speak to his gentle hearing kind commends.

[NORTHUMBERLAND *retires to* BOLINGBROKE.

[*To* AUMERLE.] We do debase ourself, cousin, do we not,
To look so poorly and to speak so fair?
Shall we call back Northumberland and send
Defiance to the traitor, and so die? 130

Aumerle. No, good my lord; let's fight with gentle words,

105–6 i.e. the tomb of Edward III, in Westminster Abbey. 108 **head:** source; cf. I. i. 97. 112 **scope:** purpose (the original meaning, from Gr. σκόπος). 113 **lineal:** hereditary. **royalties:** cf. II. i. 191. 114 **Enfranchisement:** restoration of his rights (in Bolingbroke's case, the entering into possession of his heritage). 115 **party:** side, cf. III. ii. 203. 117 **barbed:** equipped with protective 'barbes', i.e. coverings for the flanks and breast.

Till time lend friends and friends their helpful swords.
K. Rich. O God! O God! that e'er this tongue of mine,
That laid the sentence of dread banishment
On yond proud man, should take it off again 135
With words of sooth. O! that I were as great
As is my grief, or lesser than my name,
Or that I could forget what I have been,
Or not remember what I must be now.
Swell'st thou, proud heart? I'll give thee scope to beat,
Since foes have scope to beat both thee and me. 141
Aumerle. Northumberland comes back from Bolingbroke.
K. Rich. What must the king do now? Must he submit?
The king shall do it: must he be depos'd?
The king shall be contented: must he lose 145
The name of king? o' God's name, let it go:
I'll give my jewels for a set of beads,
My gorgeous palace for a hermitage,
My gay apparel for an almsman's gown,
My figur'd goblets for a dish of wood, 150
My sceptre for a palmer's walking-staff,
My subjects for a pair of carved saints,
And my large kingdom for a little grave,
A little little grave, an obscure grave;
Or I'll be buried in the king's highway, 155
Some way of common trade, where subjects' feet
May hourly trample on their sovereign's head;
For on my heart they tread now whilst I live;
And buried once, why not upon my head?
Aumerle, thou weep'st, my tender-hearted cousin! 160

136 **sooth:** flattery (usually = 'truth'; but compare the verb 'soothe'). [*N*]. 140–1 **scope:** room, opportunity (the modern sense, cf. l. 112). 147 **set of beads:** a rosary. 150 **figur'd:** engraved. 151 **palmer:** pilgrim, 'One who bore a palm branch in memory of having been to the Holy Land' (Skeat). 156 **trade:** traffic.

We'll make foul weather with despised tears;
Our sighs and they shall lodge the summer corn,
And make a dearth in this revolting land.
Or shall we play the wantons with our woes,
And make some pretty match with shedding tears? 165
As thus; to drop them still upon one place,
Till they have fretted us a pair of graves
Within the earth; and, there inlaid: 'There lies
Two kinsmen digg'd their graves with weeping eyes.'
Would not this ill do well? Well, well, I see 170
I talk but idly and you laugh at me.
Most mighty prince, my Lord Northumberland,
What says King Bolingbroke? will his majesty
Give Richard leave to live till Richard die?
You make a leg, and Bolingbroke says ay. 175

Northumberland. My lord, in the base court he doth attend
To speak with you; may't please you to come down?

K. Rich. Down, down, I come; like glistering Phaethon,
Wanting the manage of unruly jades.
In the base court? Base court, where kings grow base,
To come at traitors' calls and do them grace. 181
In the base court? Come down? Down, court! down, king!
For night-owls shriek where mounting larks should sing.
[*Exeunt from above.*

Bolingbroke. What says his majesty?

162 **lodge:** beat down. 163 **revolting:** i.e. against its king. 164 **play the wantons:** make sport of, use lightly. 165 **make some . . . match:** vie with one another. 166 **still:** always. 167 **fretted:** worn away, hollowed out. 168 **there inlaid:** when we were laid in there. [*N*]. 169 **digg'd:** who digged. 170 Would not our misfortune provide a pretty epitaph. 175 **make a leg:** bow or curtsy (in sign of assent). 176 **base court:** outer and lower court where the offices and stables were. [*N*]. 179 **Wanting the manage:** unable to control. [*N*]. 180 **grow base:** abase themselves. 183 **i.e. all is ill-omened here.**

Northumberland. Sorrow and grief of heart
Makes him speak fondly, like a frantic man: 185
Yet he is come.

Enter KING RICHARD, *and his* Attendants.

Bolingbroke. Stand all apart,
And show fair duty to his majesty. [*Kneeling.*
My gracious lord,—
K. Rich. Fair cousin, you debase your princely knee 190
To make the base earth proud with kissing it:
Me rather had my heart might feel your love
Than my unpleas'd eye see your courtesy.
Up, cousin, up; your heart is up, I know,
Thus high at least, although your knee be low. 195
Bolingbroke. My gracious lord, I come but for mine own.
K. Richard. Your own is yours, and I am yours, and all.
Bolingbroke. So far be mine, my most redoubted lord,
As my true service shall deserve your love.
K. Rich. Well you deserve: they well deserve to have
That know the strong'st and surest way to get. 201
Uncle, give me your hand: nay, dry your eyes;
Tears show their love, but want their remedies.
Cousin, I am too young to be your father,
Though you are old enough to be my heir. 205
What you will have I'll give, and willing too,
For do we must what force will have us do.
Set on towards London. Cousin, is it so?
Bolingbroke. Yea, my good lord.
K. Richard. Then I must not say no.
[*Flourish. Exeunt.*

185 **fondly**: foolishly. 195 **Thus high**: i.e. pointing to his crown. 198 **redoubted**: feared. 202 **Uncle**: i.e. York. 203 **want their remedies**: do not supply any cure for the evils.

Scene IV. LANGLEY. THE DUKE OF YORK'S GARDEN

Enter the QUEEN *and two* Ladies.

Queen. What sport shall we devise here in this garden,
To drive away the heavy thought of care?
First Lady. Madam, we'll play at bowls.
Queen. 'Twill make me think the world is full of rubs,
And that my fortune runs against the bias. 5
First Lady. Madam, we'll dance.
Queen. My legs can keep no measure in delight
When my poor heart no measure keeps in grief;
Therefore, no dancing, girl; some other sport.
First Lady. Madam, we'll tell tales. 10
Queen. Of sorrow or of joy?
First Lady. Of either, madam.
Queen. Of neither, girl:
For if of joy, being altogether wanting,
It doth remember me the more of sorrow;
Or if of grief, being altogether had, 15
It adds more sorrow to my want of joy:
For what I have I need not to repeat,
And what I want it boots not to complain.
First Lady. Madam, I'll sing.
Queen. 'Tis well that thou hast cause;
But thou shouldst please me better wouldst thou weep. 20
First Lady. I could weep, madam, would it do you good.
Queen. And I could sing would weeping do me good,

4 **rubs**: impediments, and so 'vicissitudes'. 5 **bias**: the tendency of the bowl to follow a curved course, owing to its being weighted in one side. 'Rubs' might make it follow an unexpected course. 7 **measure**: a dance; cf. I. iii. 291. 8 **measure**: moderation. 15 **being . . . had**: since I have full measure of it. 18 It is no use 'sighing the lack' of what I desire, joy. 22–3 If weeping would cure my troubles, I could sing for joy in that fact, and have no need of your tears, even though they were to do me good.

And never borrow any tear of thee.
But stay, here come the gardeners:
Let's step into the shadow of these trees. 25
My wretchedness unto a row of pins,
They'll talk of state; for every one doth so
Against a change: woe is forerun with woe.
[QUEEN *and* Ladies *retire.*

Enter a Gardener *and two* Servants.

Gardener. Go, bind thou up yon dangling apricocks,
Which, like unruly children, make their sire 30
Stoop with oppression of their prodigal weight:
Give some supportance to the bending twigs;
Go thou, and like an executioner,
Cut off the heads of too fast growing sprays,
That look too lofty in our commonwealth: 35
All must be even in our government.
You thus employ'd, I will go root away
The noisome weeds, that without profit suck
The soil's fertility from wholesome flowers.

First Servant. Why should we in the compass of a pale
Keep law and form and due proportion, 41
Showing, as in a model, our firm estate,
When our sea-walled garden, the whole land,
Is full of weeds, her fairest flowers chok'd up,
Her fruit-trees all unprun'd, her hedges ruin'd, 45
Her knots disorder'd, and her wholesome herbs

26 **My wretchedness unto:** I wager my great wretchedness against the merest trifle. 28 **Against:** in anticipation of. **woe is forerun with woe:** disaster is generally preceded by anticipation of it. 29 **dangling:** because not trained against a wall, as now. 31 **prodigal:** extravagant, lavish (but here transferred from an agent to a thing). 35 **look:** combining the senses of 'appear' and 'aim'. 36 **even:** fair, level, without favouritism. 40 **compass . . . pale:** bounds of a fence or enclosure. 42 **model:** pattern. 46 **knots:** flower-beds in intricate designs

Swarming with caterpillars?

Gardener. Hold thy peace:
He that hath suffer'd this disorder'd spring
Hath now himself met with the fall of leaf;
The weeds that his broad-spreading leaves did shelter, 50
That seem'd in eating him to hold him up,
Are pluck'd up root and all by Bolingbroke;
I mean the Earl of Wiltshire, Bushy, Green.

First Servant. What! are they dead?

Gardener. They are; and Bolingbroke
Hath seiz'd the wasteful king. O! what pity is it 55
That he hath not so trimm'd and dress'd his land
As we this garden. We at time of year
Do wound the bark, the skin of our fruit-trees,
Lest, being over-proud with sap and blood,
With too much riches it confound itself: 60
Had he done so to great and growing men,
They might have liv'd to bear and he to taste
Their fruits of duty: superfluous branches
We lop away that bearing boughs may live:
Had he done so, himself had borne the crown, 65
Which waste of idle hours hath quite thrown down.

First Servant. What! think you then the king shall be depos'd?

Gardener. Depress'd he is already, and depos'd
'Tis doubt he will be: letters came last night
To a dear friend of the good Duke of York's, 70
That tell black tidings.

Queen. O! I am press'd to death through want of speaking.
[*Coming forward.*
Thou, old Adam's likeness, set to dress this garden,

49 **the fall of leaf:** his autumn or 'fall'. 57 **at time:** at the (proper) time. 59 **over-proud:** too swollen, exuberant. [*N*]. 60 **confound:** destroy. 68 **Depress'd:** brought low (*not* merely 'sad'). 69 **'Tis doubt:** it is to be feared.

How dares thy harsh rude tongue sound this unpleasing
news?
What Eve, what serpent, hath suggested thee 75
To make a second fall of cursed man?
Why dost thou say King Richard is depos'd?
Dar'st thou, thou little better thing than earth,
Divine his downfall? Say, where, when, and how
Cam'st thou by these ill tidings? speak, thou wretch. 80

Gardener. Pardon me, madam: little joy have I
To breathe these news, yet what I say is true.
King Richard, he is in the mighty hold
Of Bolingbroke; their fortunes both are weigh'd:
In your lord's scale is nothing but himself, 85
And some few vanities that make him light;
But in the balance of great Bolingbroke,
Besides himself, are all the English peers,
And with that odds he weighs King Richard down.
Post you to London and you'll find it so; 90
I speak no more than every one doth know.

Queen. Nimble mischance, that art so light of foot,
Doth not thy embassage belong to me,
And am I last that knows it? O! thou think'st
To serve me last, that I may longest keep 95
Thy sorrow in my breast. Come, ladies, go,
To meet at London London's king in woe.
What! was I born to this, that my sad look
Should grace the triumph of great Bolingbroke?
Gardener, for telling me these news of woe, 100
Pray God the plants thou graft'st may never grow.

[*Exeunt* QUEEN *and* Ladies.

75 **suggested:** incited; cf. I. i. 101. 76 i.e. to tempt a second man to fall, by prophesying the king's fall. 79 **Divine:** foretell. 83 **hold:** keeping, custody. 86 **vanities:** worthless favourites. [*N*]. 89 **odds:** advantage. 93–4 Have I not the right to hear the news first, as most nearly concerned? 99 **triumph:** triumphal procession.

Gardener. Poor queen! so that thy state might be no worse,
I would my skill were subject to thy curse.
Here did she fall a tear; here, in this place,
I'll set a bank of rue, sour herb of grace; 105
Rue, even for ruth, here shortly shall be seen,
In the remembrance of a weeping queen. [*Exeunt*.

102 **so that**: on condition that. 104 **fall**: let fall.

ACT IV

Scene I. London. Westminster Hall

The Lords spiritual on the right side of the throne: the Lords temporal on the left; the Commons below. Enter BOLINGBROKE, AUMERLE, SURREY, NORTHUMBERLAND, HENRY PERCY, FITZWATER, *another* Lord, *the* BISHOP OF CARLISLE, *the* ABBOT OF WESTMINSTER, *and* Attendants. Officers *behind with* BAGOT.

Bolingbroke. Call forth Bagot.
Now, Bagot, freely speak thy mind;
What thou dost know of noble Gloucester's death,
Who wrought it with the king, and who perform'd
The bloody office of his timeless end. 5

Bagot. Then set before my face the Lord Aumerle.

Bolingbroke. Cousin, stand forth, and look upon that man.

Bagot. My Lord Aumerle, I know your daring tongue
Scorns to unsay what once it hath deliver'd.
In that dead time when Gloucester's death was plotted, 10
I heard you say, 'Is not my arm of length,
That reacheth from the restful English court
As far as Calais, to my uncle's head?'
Amongst much other talk, that very time,
I heard you say that you had rather refuse 15
The offer of a hundred thousand crowns
Than Bolingbroke's return to England;
Adding withal, how blest this land would be

4 **wrought . . . king:** induced the king to have it done. 5 **office:** task, duty. **timeless:** untimely (the usual sense in Shakespeare). 10 **dead:** ominous, murderous. 17 Than that B. should return to England (pronounce 'Engel-and').

In this your cousin's death.
Aumerle. Princes and noble lords,
What answer shall I make to this base man? 20
Shall I so much dishonour my fair stars,
On equal terms to give him chastisement?
Either I must, or have mine honour soil'd
With the attainder of his slanderous lips.
There is my gage, the manual seal of death, 25
That marks thee out for hell: I say thou liest,
And will maintain what thou hast said is false
In thy heart-blood, though being all too base
To stain the temper of my knightly sword.
Bolingbroke. Bagot, forbear; thou shalt not take it up. 30
Aumerle. Excepting one, I would he were the best
In all this presence that hath mov'd me so.
Fitzwater. If that thy valour stand on sympathies,
There is my gage, Aumerle, in gage to thine:
By that fair sun which shows me where thou stand'st, 35
I heard thee say, and vauntingly thou spak'st it,
That thou wert cause of noble Gloucester's death.
If thou deny'st it twenty times, thou liest;
And I will turn thy falsehood to thy heart,
Where it was forged, with my rapier's point. 40
Aumerle. Thou dar'st not, coward, live to see that day.
Fitzwater. Now, by my soul, I would it were this hour.
Aumerle. Fitzwater, thou art damn'd to hell for this.
H. Percy. Aumerle, thou liest; his honour is as true

21 **fair stars:** birth. [*N*]. 24 **attainder:** accusation, disgrace. [*N*]. 25 **manual seal of death:** alluding to the seal-manual attached to a death warrant, when the sovereign had signed it. There is a quibble on 'manual' (Lat. *manus*, hand), for Aumerle would throw down his glove as gage. 31 **one:** i.e. Bolingbroke. 33 **If that . . . sympathies:** If you will not fight unless with an equal. [*N*].

In this appeal as thou art all unjust; 45
And that thou art so, there I throw my gage,
To prove it on thee to the extremest point
Of mortal breathing: seize it if thou dar'st.

Aumerle. And if I do not may my hands rot off
And never brandish more revengeful steel 50
Over the glittering helmet of my foe!

Lord. I task the earth to the like, forsworn Aumerle;
And spur thee on with full as many lies
As may be holla'd in thy treacherous ear
From sun to sun: there is my honour's pawn; 55
Engage it to the trial if thou dar'st.

Aumerle. Who sets me else? by heaven, I'll throw at all:
I have a thousand spirits in one breast,
To answer twenty thousand such as you.

Surrey. My Lord Fitzwater, I do remember well 60
The very time Aumerle and you did talk.

Fitzwater. 'Tis very true: you were in presence then;
And you can witness with me this is true.

Surrey. As false, by heaven, as heaven itself is true,

Fitzwater. Surrey, thou liest.

Surrey. Dishonourable boy! 65
That lie shall lie so heavy on my sword
That it shall render vengeance and revenge,
Till thou the lie-giver and that lie do lie
In earth as quiet as thy father's skull.
In proof whereof, there is my honour's pawn: 70
Engage it to the trial if thou dar'st.

Fitzwater. How fondly dost thou spur a forward horse!
If I dare eat, or drink, or breathe, or live,

45 **appeal**: accusation; cf. I. i. 4. 52 **task . . . like**: tax it, load it, with a similar burden, i.e. a gage. 53 **lies**: accusations of lying. 57 **Who sets me else?**: Who else sets down stakes in wager against me? **throw**: cast the dice against, and so = 'accept their challenge'. 72 **fondly**: foolishly (since needlessly).

I dare meet Surrey in a wilderness,
And spit upon him, whilst I say he lies, 75
And lies, and lies: there is my bond of faith
To tie thee to my strong correction.
As I intend to thrive in this new world,
Aumerle is guilty of my true appeal:
Besides, I heard the banish'd Norfolk say 80
That thou, Aumerle, didst send two of thy men
To execute the noble duke at Calais.
Aumerle. Some honest Christian trust me with a gage.
That Norfolk lies, here do I throw down this,
If he may be repeal'd to try his honour. 85
Bolingbroke. These differences shall all rest under gage
Till Norfolk be repeal'd: repeal'd he shall be,
And though mine enemy, restor'd again
To all his lands and signories; when he's return'd,
Against Aumerle we will enforce his trial. 90
Carlisle. That honourable day shall ne'er be seen.
Many a time hath banish'd Norfolk fought
For Jesu Christ in glorious Christian field,
Streaming the ensign of the Christian cross
Against black pagans, Turks, and Saracens; 95
And toil'd with works of war, retir'd himself
To Italy; and there at Venice gave
His body to that pleasant country's earth,
And his pure soul unto his captain Christ,
Under whose colours he had fought so long. 100
Bolingbroke. Why, bishop, is Norfolk dead?
Carlisle. As surely as I live, my lord.

74 **in a wilderness:** i.e. where no one could intervene to save either; cf. I. i. 63–6. 76 **bond of faith:** he throws down something as a second gage. 77 To compel you to suffer severe punishment at my hands. 78 **new world:** new order of things, with Bolingbroke as king. 85 **repeal'd:** recalled. 96 **toil'd:** exhausted.

Boling. Sweet peace conduct his sweet soul to the bosom
Of good old Abraham! Lords appellants,
Your differences shall all rest under gage 105
Till we assign you to your days of trial.

Enter YORK, *attended.*

York. Great Duke of Lancaster, I come to thee
From plume-pluck'd Richard; who with willing soul
Adopts thee heir, and his high sceptre yields
To the possession of thy royal hand. 110
Ascend his throne, descending now from him;
And long live Henry, of that name the fourth!

Bolingbroke. In God's name, I'll ascend the regal throne.

Carlisle. Marry, God forbid!
Worst in this royal presence may I speak, 115
Yet best beseeming me to speak the truth.
Would God that any in this noble presence
Were enough noble to be upright judge
Of noble Richard! then, true noblesse would
Learn him forbearance from so foul a wrong. 120
What subject can give sentence on his king?
And who sits here that is not Richard's subject?
Thieves are not judg'd but they are by to hear,
Although apparent guilt be seen in them;
And shall the figure of God's majesty, 125
His captain, steward, deputy elect,
Anointed, crowned, planted many years,
Be judg'd by subject and inferior breath,
And he himself not present? O! forfend it, God,

115 **Worst**: ambiguous, either (1) lowest in rank, or (2) because I do not favour this change, and this auspicious moment is hardly the time to say so. 116 **best**: i.e. because of my position as a bishop. 119 **noblesse**: nobleness (as the Folio reads). 120 **Learn**: teach (a correct use in Eliz. Eng.). **him**: whoever was noble enough. 123 **but**: unless. 124 **apparent**: manifest; cf. I. i. 13. 129 **forfend**: forbid (which Folio reads).

That in a Christian climate souls refin'd 130
Should show so heinous, black, obscene a deed.
I speak to subjects, and a subject speaks,
Stirr'd up by God thus boldly for his king.
My Lord of Hereford here, whom you call king,
Is a foul traitor to proud Hereford's king; 135
And if you crown him, let me prophesy,
The blood of English shall manure the ground
And future ages groan for this foul act;
Peace shall go sleep with Turks and infidels,
And in this seat of peace tumultuous wars 140
Shall kin with kin and kind with kind confound;
Disorder, horror, fear and mutiny
Shall here inhabit, and this land be call'd
The field of Golgotha and dead men's skulls.
O! if you rear this house against this house, 145
It will the woefullest division prove
That ever fell upon this cursed earth.
Prevent, resist it, let it not be so,
Lest child, child's children, cry against you 'woe!'

North. Well have you argu'd, sir; and, for your pains, 150
Of capital treason we arrest you here.
My Lord of Westminster, be it your charge
To keep him safely till his day of trial.
May it please you, lords, to grant the commons' suit.

Bolingbroke. Fetch hither Richard, that in common view
He may surrender; so we shall proceed 156
Without suspicion.

York. I will be his conduct. [*Exit.*

130 **climate:** region, country, cf. 'clime'. **refin'd:** i.e. by Christian training. 131 **obscene:** odious (the wider, Latin, sense, rather than the more limited modern one). 141 **kin:** family, relatives by blood. **kind:** those of the same nature, e.g. fellow-countrymen. [*N*]. 151 **Of:** on a charge of. 157 **conduct:** escort.

Bolingbroke. Lords, you that here are under our arrest,
Procure your sureties for your days of answer.
[*To* CARLISLE.] Little are we beholding to your love, 160
And little look'd for at your helping hands.

Re-enter YORK, *with* KING RICHARD, *and* Officers *bearing the Crown, &c.*

K. Richard. Alack! why am I sent for to a king
Before I have shook off the regal thoughts
Wherewith I reign'd? I hardly yet have learn'd
To insinuate, flatter, bow, and bend my limbs: 165
Give sorrow leave awhile to tutor me
To this submission. Yet I well remember
The favours of these men: were they not mine?
Did they not sometime cry, 'All hail!' to me?
So Judas did to Christ: but he, in twelve, 170
Found truth in all but one; I, in twelve thousand, none.
God save the king! Will no man say, amen?
Am I both priest and clerk? well then, amen.
God save the king! although I be not he;
And yet, amen, if heaven do think him me. 175
To do what service am I sent for hither?

York. To do that office of thine own good will
Which tired majesty did make thee offer,
The resignation of thy state and crown
To Henry Bolingbroke. 180

K. Richard. Give me the crown. Here, cousin, seize the crown;
Here cousin,
On this side my hand and on that side thine.
Now is this golden crown like a deep well
That owes two buckets filling one another; 185
The emptier ever dancing in the air,

160 **beholding**: indebted. 168 **favours**: features. 175 **amen**: so be it. 185 **owes**: owns.

The other down, unseen and full of water:
That bucket down and full of tears am I,
Drinking my griefs, whilst you mount up on high.

Boling. I thought you had been willing to resign. 190

K. Rich. My crown, I am; but still my griefs are mine.
You may my glories and my state depose,
But not my griefs; still am I king of those.

Boling. Part of your cares you give me with your crown.

K. Rich. Your cares set up do not pluck my cares down.
My care is loss of care, by old care done; 196
Your care is gain of care, by new care won,
The cares I give I have, though given away;
They tend the crown, yet still with me they stay.

Boling. Are you contented to resign the crown? 200

K. Richard. Ay, no; no, ay; for I must nothing be;
Therefore no no, for I resign to thee.
Now mark me how I will undo myself:
I give this heavy weight from off my head,
And this unwieldy sceptre from my hand, 205
The pride of kingly sway from out my heart;
With mine own tears I wash away my balm,
With mine own hands I give away my crown,
With mine own tongue deny my sacred state,
With mine own breath release all duty's rites: 210
All pomp and majesty I do forswear;
My manors, rents, revenues, I forego;
My acts, decrees, and statutes I deny:
God pardon all oaths that are broke to me!
God keep all vows unbroke are made to thee! 215

196 **done:** now finished with. [*N*]. 199 **tend:** accompany, attend upon. 203 **undo myself:** strip myself of my honours (and so reduce to nothing). 207 **balm:** consecrated oil used at the coronation; cf. III. ii. 55. 210 **duty's rites:** the ceremonious observances which subjects are bound to render to their sovereign. 215 **are:** which are; cf. l. 256 for the omission.

Make me, that nothing have, with nothing griev'd,
And thou with all pleas'd, that hast all achiev'd!
Long mayst thou live in Richard's seat to sit,
And soon lie Richard in an earthy pit!
God save King Henry, unking'd Richard says, 220
And send him many years of sunshine days!
What more remains?

North. [*Offering a paper.*] No more, but that you read
These accusations and these grievous crimes
Committed by your person and your followers
Against the state and profit of this land; 225
That, by confessing them, the souls of men
May deem that you are worthily depos'd.

K. Richard. Must I do so? and must I ravel out
My weav'd-up follies? Gentle Northumberland,
If thy offences were upon record, 230
Would it not shame thee in so fair a troop
To read a lecture of them? If thou wouldst,
There shouldst thou find one heinous article,
Containing the deposing of a king,
And cracking the strong warrant of an oath, 235
Mark'd with a blot, damn'd in the book of heaven.
Nay, all of you that stand and look upon me,
Whilst that my wretchedness doth bait myself,
Though some of you with Pilate wash your hands,
Showing an outward pity; yet you Pilates 240
Have here deliver'd me to my sour cross,
And water cannot wash away your sin.

North. My lord, dispatch; read o'er these articles.

225 **state and profit:** settled order and progress. 228 **ravel out:** unravel, disentangle. 231 **troop:** assembly. 232 **read a lecture:** make a public discourse or sermon. 238 **bait:** i.e. Richard is the bear tied to the stake, his wretchedness the dogs which 'bait' or worry it for the amusement of the spectators. 241 **sour:** bitter. 243 **dispatch:** make haste.

K. Richard. Mine eyes are full of tears, I cannot see:
And yet salt water blinds them not so much 245
But they can see a sort of traitors here.
Nay, if I turn mine eyes upon myself,
I find myself a traitor with the rest;
For I have given here my soul's consent
To undeck the pompous body of a king; 250
Made glory base and sovereignty a slave,
Proud majesty a subject, state a peasant.

Northumberland. My lord,—

K. Richard. No lord of thine, thou haught insulting man,
Nor no man's lord; I have no name, no title, 255
No, not that name was given me at the font,
But 'tis usurp'd: alack the heavy day!
That I have worn so many winters out,
And know not now what name to call myself.
O! that I were a mockery king of snow, 260
Standing before the sun of Bolingbroke,
To melt myself away in water-drops.
Good king, great king,—and yet not greatly good,
An if my word be sterling yet in England,
Let it command a mirror hither straight, 265
That it may show me what a face I have,
Since it is bankrupt of his majesty.

Bolingbroke. Go some of you and fetch a looking-glass.
[*Exit an* Attendant.

North. Read o'er this paper while the glass doth come.

K. Richard. Fiend! thou torment'st me ere I come to hell. 270

246 **sort:** set, crew (nearly always in contempt). 250 **pompous:** clothed in splendour (without the modern meaning). 254 **haught:** haughty. 257 **usurp'd:** i.e. he who had taken the crown had taken all that was Richard's by right of birth. 264 **An if . . . sterling:** if it be that my word has its proper value (like good coin); cf. I. iii. 231. 267 **his:** its.

Bolingbroke. Urge it no more, my Lord Northumberland.
Northumberland. The commons will not then be satisfied.
K. Richard. They shall be satisfied: I'll read enough
When I do see the very book indeed
Where all my sins are writ, and that's myself. 275

Re-enter Attendant, *with a glass.*

Give me the glass, and therein will I read.
No deeper wrinkles yet? Hath sorrow struck
So many blows upon this face of mine
And made no deeper wounds? O, flattering glass!
Like to my followers in prosperity, 280
Thou dost beguile me. Was this face the face
That every day under his household roof
Did keep ten thousand men? Was this the face
That like the sun did make beholders wink?
Was this the face that fac'd so many follies, 285
And was at last out-fac'd by Bolingbroke?
A brittle glory shineth in this face:
As brittle as the glory is the face;
[*Dashes the glass against the ground.*
For there it is, crack'd in a hundred shivers.
Mark, silent king, the moral of this sport, 290
How soon my sorrow hath destroy'd my face.
Bolingbroke. The shadow of your sorrow hath destroy'd
The shadow of your face.
K. Richard. Say that again.
The shadow of my sorrow! Ha! let's see:
'Tis very true, my grief lies all within; 295
And these external manners of laments
Are merely shadows to the unseen grief

285 **fac'd**: committed boldly (and also perhaps 'gave lustre to'). 286 **out-fac'd**: outshone, browbeaten. 292 **The shadow of your sorrow**: an affected, unreal sorrow. 293 **The shadow of your face**: i.e. in the mirror.

That swells with silence in the tortur'd soul;
There lies the substance: and I thank thee, king,
For thy great bounty, that not only giv'st 300
Me cause to wail, but teachest me the way
How to lament the cause. I'll beg one boon,
And then be gone and trouble you no more.
Shall I obtain it?

Bolingbroke. Name it, fair cousin.

K. Richard. 'Fair cousin!' I am greater than a king; 305
For when I was a king, my flatterers
Were then but subjects; being now a subject,
I have a king here to my flatterer.
Being so great, I have no need to beg.

Bolingbroke. Yet ask. 310

K. Richard. And shall I have?

Bolingbroke. You shall.

K. Richard. Then give me leave to go.

Bolingbroke. Whither? 314

K. Richard. Whither you will, so I were from your sights.

Bolingbroke. Go, some of you convey him to the Tower.

K. Richard. O, good! convey? conveyers are you all,
That rise thus nimbly by a true king's fall.

[*Exeunt* KING RICHARD *and* Guard.

Bolingbroke. On Wednesday next we solemnly set down
Our coronation: lords, prepare yourselves. 320

[*Exeunt all except the* BISHOP OF CARLISLE, *the* ABBOT OF WESTMINSTER, *and* AUMERLE.

Abbot. A woeful pageant have we here beheld.

Bishop. The woe's to come; the children yet unborn
Shall feel this day as sharp to them as thorn.

Aumerle. You holy clergymen, is there no plot
To rid the realm of this pernicious blot? 325

Abbot. My lord,

308 **to**: as, for, cf. 'take to wife'. 317 **conveyers**: thieves. [*N*].
319 **set down**: determine.

Before I freely speak my mind herein,
You shall not only take the sacrament
To bury mine intents, but also to effect
Whatever I shall happen to devise. 330
I see your brows are full of discontent,
Your hearts of sorrow, and your eyes of tears:
Come home with me to supper; I will lay
A plot shall show us all a merry day. [*Exeunt.*

ACT V

Scene I. London. A Street leading to the Tower

Enter the Queen *and* Ladies.

Queen. This way the king will come; this is the way
To Julius Cæsar's ill-erected tower,
To whose flint bosom my condemned lord
Is doom'd a prisoner by proud Bolingbroke.
Here let us rest, if this rebellious earth 5
Have any resting for her true king's queen.

Enter King Richard *and* Guard.

But soft, but see, or rather do not see,
My fair rose wither: yet look up, behold,
That you in pity may dissolve to dew,
And wash him fresh again with true-love tears. 10
Ah! thou, the model where old Troy did stand,
Thou map of honour, thou King Richard's tomb,
And not King Richard; thou most beauteous inn,
Why should hard-favour'd grief be lodg'd in thee,
When triumph is become an alehouse guest? 15

K. Richard. Join not with grief, fair woman, do not so,
To make my end too sudden: learn, good soul,
To think our former state a happy dream;
From which awak'd, the truth of what we are
Shows us but this. I am sworn brother, sweet, 20
To grim Necessity, and he and I

2 **ill-erected:** erected either (1) for an evil purpose, or (2) under evil auspices (since her husband is to be imprisoned there). 3 **flint:** stony, hard. 7 **soft:** hush, stop. 11 **thou:** Richard, *not* the Tower. [*N*]. 20 **Shows us but:** reveals that we are only. [*N*].

Will keep a league till death. Hie thee to France,
And cloister thee in some religious house:
Our holy lives must win a new world's crown,
Which our profane hours here have stricken down. 25

Queen. What! is my Richard both in shape and mind
Transform'd and weaken'd! Hath Bolingbroke depos'd
Thine intellect? hath he been in thy heart?
The lion dying thrusteth forth his paw
And wounds the earth, if nothing else, with rage 30
To be o'erpower'd; and wilt thou, pupil-like,
Take thy correction mildly, kiss the rod,
And fawn on rage with base humility,
Which art a lion and a king of beasts?

K. Rich. A king of beasts indeed; if aught but beasts, 35
I had been still a happy king of men.
Good sometime queen, prepare thee hence for France,
Think I am dead, and that even here thou tak'st,
As from my death-bed, my last living leave.
In winter's tedious nights sit by the fire 40
With good old folks, and let them tell thee tales
Of woeful ages, long ago betid;
And ere thou bid good night, to quit their grief,
Tell thou the lamentable tale of me,
And send the hearers weeping to their beds: 45
For why the senseless brands will sympathize
The heavy accent of thy moving tongue,
And in compassion weep the fire out;

24–5 'We must win by a religious life that heavenly crown which we have lost by our previous sinful hours.' 31 **To be**: at being. 35 **if aught but beasts**: if my subjects were anything but beasts. 37 **sometime**: former, quondam. **hence**: either (1) to go hence, or (2) henceforward. 39 **last living leave**: last leave of me alive. 42 **betid**: that happened (with 'tales'). 43 **to quit . . . grief**: as a return for their stories of affliction. 46 **sympathize**: show responsive feeling to. 48 **compassion**: four syllables (*or* 'fire' two syllables).

And some will mourn in ashes, some coal-black,
For the deposing of a rightful king. 50

Enter NORTHUMBERLAND, *attended.*

North. My lord, the mind of Bolingbroke is chang'd;
You must to Pomfret, not unto the Tower.
And, madam, there is order ta'en for you;
With all swift speed you must away to France.
K. Rich. Northumberland, thou ladder wherewithal 55
The mounting Bolingbroke ascends my throne,
The time shall not be many hours of age
More than it is, ere foul sin gathering head
Shall break into corruption. Thou shalt think,
Though he divide the realm and give thee half, 60
It is too little, helping him to all;
And he shall think that thou, which know'st the way
To plant unrightful kings, wilt know again,
Being ne'er so little urg'd, another way
To pluck him headlong from the usurped throne. 65
The love of wicked friends converts to fear;
That fear to hate, and hate turns one or both
To worthy danger and deserved death.
North. My guilt be on my head, and there an end.
Take leave and part; for you must part forthwith. 70
K. Richard. Doubly divorc'd! Bad men, ye violate
A two-fold marriage; 'twixt my crown and me,
And then, betwixt me and my married wife.
Let me unkiss the oath 'twixt thee and me;
And yet not so, for with a kiss 'twas made. 75

53 **order ta'en**: provision or arrangement made. 61 **helping . . . all**: since by your help he secured all (an absolute construction). 66 **converts**: changes (*intrans.*). 67 **turns**: brings. 68 **worthy**: merited. 69 **and there an end**: and there's an end, that is all I have to say. 74 **unkiss**: unmake with a kiss (on the *false* analogy of 'undo', &c., hence 'not so', l. 75).

Part us, Northumberland: I towards the north,
Where shivering cold and sickness pines the clime;
My wife to France: from whence, set forth in pomp.
She came adorned hither like sweet May,
Sent back like Hallowmas or short'st of day. 80

Queen. And must we be divided? must we part?

K. Richard. Ay, hand from hand, my love, and heart from heart.

Queen. Banish us both and send the king with me.

Northumberland. That were some love but little policy.

Queen. Then whither he goes, thither let me go. 85

K. Richard. So two, together weeping, make one woe.
Weep thou for me in France, I for thee here;
Better far off, than near, be ne'er the near.
Go, count thy way with sighs, I mine with groans.

Queen. So longest way shall have the longest moans. 90

K. Richard. Twice for one step I'll groan, the way being short,
And piece the way out with a heavy heart.
Come, come, in wooing sorrow let's be brief,
Since, wedding it, there is such length in grief.
One kiss shall stop our mouths, and dumbly part; 95
Thus give I mine, and thus take I thy heart. [*They kiss.*

Queen. Give me mine own again; 'twere no good part
To take on me to keep and kill thy heart. [*They kiss again.*
So, now I have mine own again, be gone,
That I may strive to kill it with a groan. 100

K. Richard. We make woe wanton with this fond delay:
Once more, adieu; the rest let sorrow say. [*Exeunt.*

77 **pines:** makes to pine, afflicts (transitive only here in Shakespeare). 88 **Better far . . . near:** better be a long way apart, than near and never able to meet. (The second 'near' = 'nearer', cf. III. ii. 64). 92 **piece the way out:** make it appear longer, so as to equal her journey. (There might be a quibble on 'pace'.) 95 **part:** separate us. 96 **mine:** i.e. my heart. 101 **wanton:** unrestrained, self-indulgent; cf. III. iii. 164.

Scene II. The Same. A Room in the Duke of York's Palace

Enter YORK *and his* DUCHESS.

Duchess. My lord, you told me you would tell the rest,
When weeping made you break the story off,
Of our two cousins coming into London.
York. Where did I leave?
Duchess. At that sad stop, my lord,
Where rude misgovern'd hands, from windows' tops, 5
Threw dust and rubbish on King Richard's head.
York. Then, as I said, the duke, great Bolingbroke,
Mounted upon a hot and fiery steed,
Which his aspiring rider seem'd to know,
With slow but stately pace kept on his course, 10
While all tongues cried, 'God save thee, Bolingbroke!'
You would have thought the very windows spake,
So many greedy looks of young and old
Through casements darted their desiring eyes
Upon his visage, and that all the walls 15
With painted imagery had said at once
'Jesu preserve thee! welcome, Bolingbroke!'
Whilst he, from one side to the other turning,
Bare-headed, lower than his proud steed's neck,
Bespake them thus, 'I thank you, countrymen:' 20
And thus still doing, thus he pass'd along.
Duchess. Alack, poor Richard! where rode he the whilst?
York. As in a theatre, the eyes of men,
After a well-grac'd actor leaves the stage,
Are idly bent on him that enters next, 25

9 Which seemed to know the ambitious nature of its rider. (Cf. v. v. 78–84.) 12–17 'The windows were so crowded with people that they seemed to be alive, and the walls so hung with mottoed tapestries that they seemed to cry "Welcome!"' [*N*].
25 **idly:** with indifference.

Thinking his prattle to be tedious;
Even so, or with much more contempt, men's eyes
Did scowl on Richard: no man cried, 'God save him;'
No joyful tongue gave him his welcome home;
But dust was thrown upon his sacred head, 30
Which with such gentle sorrow he shook off,
His face still combating with tears and smiles,
The badges of his grief and patience,
That had not God, for some strong purpose, steel'd
The hearts of men, they must perforce have melted, 35
And barbarism itself have pitied him.
But heaven hath a hand in these events,
To whose high will we bound our calm contents.
To Bolingbroke are we sworn subjects now,
Whose state and honour I for aye allow. 40

Duchess. Here comes my son Aumerle.

York. Aumerle that was;
But that is lost for being Richard's friend,
And, madam, you must call him Rutland now.
I am in parliament pledge for his truth
And lasting fealty to the new-made king. 45

Enter AUMERLE.

Duchess. Welcome, my son: who are the violets now
That strew the green lap of the new-come spring?

Aumerle. Madam, I know not, nor I greatly care not:
God knows I had as lief be none as one.

York. Well, bear you well in this new spring of time, 50
Lest you be cropp'd before you come to prime.
What news from Oxford? hold those justs and triumphs?

32 **combating with:** showing the struggle going on between; cf. III. ii. 10, 'weeping, smiling'. 38 **To whose . . . contents:** Whose will we accept and wish nothing further. [*N*]. 40 **allow:** admit. 46–7 Who are the new king's favourites? 49 **I had as lief:** I would as willingly. 52 **hold . . . triumphs?:** are those suggested tournaments and shows to be held?

Aumerle. For aught I know, my lord, they do.
York. You will be there, I know.
Aumerle. If God prevent it not, I purpose so. 55
York. What seal is that that hangs without thy bosom?
Yea, look'st thou pale? let me see the writing.
Aumerle. My lord, 'tis nothing.
York. No matter then, who sees it:
I will be satisfied; let me see the writing.
Aumerle. I do beseech your Grace to pardon me: 60
It is a matter of small consequence,
Which for some reasons I would not have seen.
York. Which for some reasons, sir, I mean to see.
I fear, I fear,—
Duchess. What should you fear?
'Tis nothing but some band he's enter'd into 65
For gay apparel 'gainst the triumph day.
York. Bound to himself! what doth he with a bond
That he is bound to? Wife, thou art a fool.
Boy, let me see the writing.
Aumerle. I do beseech you, pardon me; I may not show it.
York. I will be satisfied; let me see it, I say. 71
[*Snatches it, and reads.*
Treason! foul treason! villain! traitor! slave!
Duchess. What is the matter, my lord?
York. Ho! who is within there?

Enter a Servant.

Saddle my horse.
God for his mercy! what treachery is here! 75
Duchess. Why, what is it, my lord?
York. Give me my boots, I say; saddle my horse.

60 **pardon me**: excuse me (from showing it). 65 **band**: bond (which Folio reads); cf. I. i. 2. 66 **'gainst**: in anticipation of; cf. III. iv. 28. 67–8 i.e. if Aumerle had given a bond to some one, that person, not he, would keep the bond.

Now, by mine honour, by my life, my troth,
I will appeach the villain. [*Exit* Servant.
Duchess. What's the matter?
York. Peace, foolish woman. 80
Duchess. I will not peace. What is the matter, Aumerle?
Aumerle. Good mother, be content; it is no more
Than my poor life must answer.
Duchess. Thy life answer!
York. Bring me my boots: I will unto the king. 84

Re-enter Servant *with boots.*

Duchess. Strike him, Aumerle. Poor boy, thou art amaz'd.
[*To* Servant.] Hence, villain! never come more in my sight.
[*Exit* Servant.
York. Give me my boots, I say.
Duchess. Why, York, what wilt thou do?
Wilt thou not hide the trespass of thine own?
Have we more sons, or are we like to have? 90
Is not my teeming date drunk up with time?
And wilt thou pluck my fair son from mine age,
And rob me of a happy mother's name?
Is he not like thee? is he not thine own?
York. Thou fond, mad woman, 95
Wilt thou conceal this dark conspiracy?
A dozen of them here have ta'en the sacrament,
And interchangeably set down their hands,
To kill the king at Oxford.
Duchess. He shall be none;
We'll keep him here: then, what is that to him? 100
York. Away, fond woman! were he twenty times

79 **appeach**: inform against, denounce. 83 **answer**: answer for. 85 **amaz'd**: bewildered, distracted; cf. I. iii. 81. 91 Has not my time for bearing children passed? 92 **age**: old age. 97 **ta'en the sacrament**: sworn on the Eucharist. 98 **interchangeably**: in exchange (for the signatures of the others). 99 **none**: i.e. not one of the conspirators.

My son, I would appeach him.
Duchess. Hadst thou groan'd for him
As I have done, thou'dst be more pitiful.
But now I know thy mind: thou dost suspect
That I have been disloyal to thy bed, 105
And that he is a bastard, not thy son:
Sweet York, sweet husband, be not of that mind:
He is as like thee as a man may be,
Not like to me, nor any of my kin,
And yet I love him.
York. Make way, unruly woman! [*Exit.* 110
Duchess. After, Aumerle! Mount thee upon his horse;
Spur post, and get before him to the king,
And beg thy pardon ere he do accuse thee.
I'll not be long behind; though I be old,
I doubt not but to ride as fast as York: 115
And never will I rise up from the ground
Till Bolingbroke have pardon'd thee. Away! be gone.
[*Exeunt.*

Scene III. WINDSOR. A ROOM IN THE CASTLE

Enter BOLINGBROKE *as King*; HENRY PERCY, *and other* Lords.

Bolingbroke. Can no man tell of my unthrifty son?
'Tis full three months since I did see him last.
If any plague hang over us, 'tis he.
I would to God, my lords, he might be found:
Inquire at London, 'mongst the taverns there, 5
For there, they say, he daily doth frequent,
With unrestrained loose companions,

111 After: go after him. **112 post:** in haste (used as adverb).
1 unthrifty: good for nothing. **7 companions:** in Eliz. Eng. often used in depreciatory sense.

Even such, they say, as stand in narrow lanes
And beat our watch and rob our passengers;
While he, young wanton and effeminate boy, 10
Takes on the point of honour to support
So dissolute a crew.

H. Percy. My lord, some two days since I saw the prince,
And told him of these triumphs held at Oxford.

Bolingbroke. And what said the gallant? 15

H. Percy. His answer was: he would unto the stews,
And from the common'st creature pluck a glove,
And wear it as a favour; and with that
He would unhorse the lustiest challenger.

Boling. As dissolute as desperate; yet, through both, 20
I see some sparkles of a better hope,
Which elder days may happily bring forth.
But who comes here?

Enter AUMERLE.

Aumerle. Where is the king?

Bolingbroke. What means
Our cousin, that he stares and looks so wildly? 25

Aum. God save your Grace! I do beseech your majesty,
To have some conference with your Grace alone.

Boling. Withdraw yourselves, and leave us here alone.
[*Exeunt* H. PERCY *and* Lords.
What is the matter with our cousin now?

Aumerle. [*Kneels.*] For ever may my knees grow to the earth, 30
My tongue cleave to my roof within my mouth,
Unless a pardon ere I rise or speak.

Bolingbroke. Intended or committed was this fault?

14 **triumphs**: see v. ii. 52. 16 **the stews**: places of ill fame.
22 **happily**: probably here = haply, perchance.

If on the first, how heinous e'er it be,
To win thy after-love I pardon thee. 35

Aumerle. Then give me leave that I may turn the key,
That no man enter till my tale be done.

Bolingbroke. Have thy desire.

[AUMERLE *locks the door.*

York. [*Within.*] My liege, beware! look to thyself;
Thou hast a traitor in thy presence there. 40

Bolingbroke. [*Drawing.*] Villain, I'll make thee safe.

Aumerle. Stay thy revengeful hand; thou hast no cause to fear.

York. [*Within.*] Open the door, secure, fool-hardy king:
Shall I for love speak treason to thy face?
Open the door, or I will break it open. 45

[BOLINGBROKE *unlocks the door; and afterwards re-locks it.*

Enter YORK.

Bolingbroke. What is the matter, uncle? speak;
Recover breath; tell us how near is danger,
That we may arm us to encounter it.

York. Peruse this writing here, and thou shalt know
The treason that my haste forbids me show. 50

Aum. Remember, as thou read'st, thy promise pass'd:
I do repent me; read not my name there;
My heart is not confederate with my hand.

York. 'Twas, villain, ere thy hand did set it down.
I tore it from the traitor's bosom, king; 55
Fear, and not love, begets his penitence.
Forget to pity him, lest thy pity prove
A serpent that will sting thee to the heart.

34 **on the first**: in the former category. 41 **safe**: unable to hurt me. 43 **secure**: over-confident. 44 Will you make me, through my concern for your safety, describe your conduct in such treasonable terms?

Bolingbroke. O heinous, strong, and bold conspiracy!
O loyal father of a treacherous son! 60
Thou sheer, immaculate, and silver fountain,
From whence this stream through muddy passages
Hath held his current and defil'd himself!
Thy overflow of good converts to bad,
And thy abundant goodness shall excuse 65
This deadly blot in thy digressing son.

York. So shall my virtue be his vice's bawd,
And he shall spend mine honour with his shame,
As thriftless sons their scraping fathers' gold.
Mine honour lives when his dishonour dies, 70
Or my sham'd life in his dishonour lies:
Thou kill'st me in his life; giving him breath,
The traitor lives, the true man's put to death.

Duchess. [*Within.*] What ho, my liege! for God's sake let me in.

Bolingbroke. What shrill-voic'd suppliant makes this eager cry? 75

Duchess. [*Within.*] A woman, and thine aunt, great king; 'tis I.
Speak with me, pity me, open the door:
A beggar begs, that never begg'd before.

Bolingbroke. Our scene is alter'd from a serious thing,
And now chang'd to 'The Beggar and the King.' 80
My dangerous cousin, let your mother in:

61 **sheer**: pure, perfect. 62 **this stream**: i.e. Aumerle, deriving his being from York as source or fountain. 64 Your excess of goodness has a bad effect (for it persuades us to pardon your son). **converts**: is transformed; cf. v. i. 66. 66 **digressing**: transgressing. 67 **be his vice's bawd**: pander to, provide for, his vice. 68 **spend mine honour**: use up the fund of honour I have accumulated. 69 **thriftless**: wasteful. 70–3 My honour is revived when his dishonour ends, i.e. when he is executed; if you let him live, you kill me. Line 71 would be simpler if one read 'For . . .'

I know she's come to pray for your foul sin.
[AUMERLE *unlocks the door.*

York. If thou do pardon, whosoever pray,
More sins, for this forgiveness, prosper may.
This fester'd joint cut off, the rest rests sound; 85
This, let alone, will all the rest confound.

Enter DUCHESS.

Duchess. O king! believe not this hard-hearted man:
Love, loving not itself, none other can.

York. Thou frantic woman, what dost thou make here?
Shall thy old dugs once more a traitor rear? 90

Duchess. Sweet York, be patient. [*Kneels.*
Hear me, gentle liege.

Bolingbroke. Rise up, good aunt.

Duchess. Not yet, I thee beseech.
For ever will I walk upon my knees,
And never see day that the happy sees,
Till thou give joy; until thou bid me joy, 95
By pardoning Rutland, my transgressing boy.

Aumerle. Unto my mother's prayers I bend my knee.
[*Kneels.*

York. Against them both my true joints bended be.
[*Kneels.*
Ill mayst thou thrive if thou grant any grace!

Duchess. Pleads he in earnest? look upon his face; 100
His eyes do drop no tears, his prayers are in jest;
His words come from his mouth, ours from our breast:

83–4 'If you pardon Aumerle, no matter at whose entreaty, other traitors will flourish.' 85 **This fester'd joint:** *if* this . . . (and so in l. 86). **the rest:** of the body politic. 88 i.e. If York cannot love Aumerle, his own flesh and blood, how can he profess to love anything else—for instance, the king? 89 **make:** do. 90 **rear:** raise up. 94 **the happy:** the happy person. 97 **Unto:** in support of, in addition to.

He prays but faintly and would be denied;
We pray with heart and soul and all beside:
His weary joints would gladly rise, I know; 105
Our knees shall kneel till to the ground they grow:
His prayers are full of false hypocrisy;
Ours of true zeal and deep integrity.
Our prayers do out-pray his; then let them have
That mercy which true prayer ought to have. 110

Bolingbroke. Good aunt, stand up.

Duchess. Nay, do not say 'stand up;'
But 'pardon' first, and afterwards 'stand up.'
An if I were thy nurse, thy tongue to teach,
'Pardon' should be the first word of thy speech.
I never long'd to hear a word till now; 115
Say 'pardon,' king; let pity teach thee how:
The word is short, but not so short as sweet;
No word like 'pardon' for kings' mouths so meet.

York. Speak it in French, king; say, '*pardonnez moy.*'

Duchess. Dost thou teach pardon pardon to destroy? 120
Ah! my sour husband, my hard-hearted lord,
That sett'st the word itself against the word.
Speak 'pardon' as 'tis current in our land;
The chopping French we do not understand.
Thine eye begins to speak, set thy tongue there, 125
Or in thy piteous heart plant thou thine ear,
That hearing how our plaints and prayers do pierce,
Pity may move thee pardon to rehearse.

Bolingbroke. Good aunt, stand up.

Duchess. I do not sue to stand;

103 **would be**: would willingly be, desires to be. 113 **An if**: if. 119 **pardonnez moy**: excuse me, i.e. a polite refusal. 124 **chopping**: probably 'changing the meaning of words'. [*N*]. 125–6 Let your tongue express the pity your eye reveals, or your ear listen to your heart (not to what others say). 128 **rehearse**: pronounce, say aloud.

Pardon is all the suit I have in hand. 130

Bolingbroke. I pardon him, as God shall pardon me.

Duchess. O happy vantage of a kneeling knee!
Yet am I sick for fear: speak it again;
Twice saying 'pardon' doth not pardon twain,
But makes one pardon strong.

Bolingbroke. With all my heart 135
I pardon him.

Duchess. A god on earth thou art.

Boling. But for our trusty brother-in-law and the abbot,
With all the rest of that consorted crew,
Destruction straight shall dog them at the heels.
Good uncle, help to order several powers 140
To Oxford, or where'er these traitors are:
They shall not live within this world, I swear,
But I will have them, if I once know where.
Uncle, farewell: and cousin too, adieu:
Your mother well hath pray'd, and prove you true. 145

Duchess. Come, my old son: I pray God make thee new.

[*Exeunt.*

Scene IV. Another Room in the Castle

Enter EXTON *and a* Servant.

Exton. Didst thou not mark the king, what words he spake?
'Have I no friend will rid me of this living fear?'
Was it not so?

Servant. Those were his very words.

Exton. 'Have I no friend?' quoth he: he spake it twice,

132 **vantage:** a happy combination of 'benefit', 'profit', with the idea of 'point or position of vantage', i.e. superior position, in military affairs. 138 **consorted:** confederate; cf. v. vi. 15. 140 **order several powers:** marshal and set going distinct bodies of troops.

And urg'd it twice together, did he not? 5
Servant. He did.
Exton. And speaking it, he wistly looked on me,
As who should say, 'I would thou wert the man
That would divorce this terror from my heart;'
Meaning the king at Pomfret. Come, let's go: 10
I am the king's friend, and will rid his foe. [*Exeunt.*

Scene V. POMFRET. THE DUNGEON OF THE CASTLE

Enter KING RICHARD.

K. Richard. I have been studying how I may compare
This prison where I live unto the world:
And for because the world is populous,
And here is not a creature but myself,
I cannot do it; yet I'll hammer it out. 5
My brain I'll prove the female to my soul;
My soul the father: and these two beget
A generation of still-breeding thoughts,
And these same thoughts people this little world
In humours like the people of this world, 10
For no thought is contented. The better sort,
As thoughts of things divine, are intermix'd
With scruples, and do set the word itself
Against the word:
As thus, 'Come, little ones;' and then again, 15

5 **urg'd:** see III. i. 4. 7 **wistly:** wistfully. 8 **As who should say:** as if his looks meant. 9 **divorce:** separate, drive away. 11 **rid:** remove.

8 **generation:** family, progeny. **still-breeding:** that go on breeding. 9 **this little world:** i.e. probably the prison, but possibly his mind. [*N*]. 10 **humours:** dispositions, natures. [*N*]. Thoughts, Richard says, are like people; they are dissatisfied. 12 **As . . . divine:** namely, religious thoughts. 13 **scruples:** doubts, dilemmas. **the word:** Scripture; cf. v. iii. 122.

'It is as hard to come as for a camel
To thread the postern of a needle's eye.'
Thoughts tending to ambition, they do plot
Unlikely wonders: how these vain weak nails
May tear a passage through the flinty ribs 20
Of this hard world, my ragged prison walls;
And, for they cannot, die in their own pride.
Thoughts tending to content flatter themselves
That they are not the first of fortune's slaves,
Nor shall not be the last; like silly beggars 25
Who sitting in the stocks refuge their shame,
That many have and others must sit there:
And in this thought they find a kind of ease,
Bearing their own misfortune on the back
Of such as have before endur'd the like. 30
Thus play I in one person many people,
And none contented: sometimes am I king;
Then treason makes me wish myself a beggar,
And so I am: then crushing penury
Persuades me I was better when a king; 35
Then am I king'd again; and by and by
Think that I am unking'd by Bolingbroke,
And straight am nothing: but whate'er I be,
Nor I nor any man that but man is
With nothing shall be pleas'd, till he be eas'd 40
With being nothing. Music do I hear? [*Music.*
Ha, ha! keep time. How sour sweet music is
When time is broke and no proportion kept!
So is it in the music of men's lives.

17 **thread:** make one's way through. **postern:** small gate.
20 **ribs:** walls. 21 **ragged:** rugged. 25 **silly:** simple.
26–7 **refuge . . . That:** solace their shame, by thinking that . . .
29 Unloading their misfortune on to such . . . 39–41 i.e. Neither I nor any mere mortal will ever be satisfied with anything this side of the grave. 43 **proportion:** i.e. 'between the time spent in dwelling on successive notes' (Chambers).

And here have I the daintiness of ear 45
To check time broke in a disorder'd string;
But for the concord of my state and time
Had not an ear to hear my true time broke.
I wasted time, and now doth time waste me;
For now hath time made me his numbering clock: 50
My thoughts are minutes, and with sighs they jar
Their watches on unto mine eyes, the outward watch,
Whereto my finger, like a dial's point,
Is pointing still, in cleansing them from tears.
Now sir, the sound that tells what hour it is 55
Are clamorous groans, that strike upon my heart
Which is the bell: so sighs and tears and groans
Show minutes, times, and hours; but my time
Runs posting on in Bolingbroke's proud joy,
While I stand fooling here, his Jack o' the clock. 60
This music mads me: let it sound no more;
For though it have holp madmen to their wits,
In me it seems it will make wise men mad.
Yet blessing on his heart that gives it me!
For 'tis a sign of love, and love to Richard 65
Is a strange brooch in this all-hating world.

Enter Groom of the Stable.

Groom. Hail, royal prince!
K. Richard. Thanks, noble peer;

46 To object to bad time in a faulty musical instrument. 47 But as regards the harmony of my kingdom and age. 50 **numbering clock:** with which he records time's passage by the number of the hours and minutes. 51–2 **jar Their watches on:** i.e. make the jerky movement at each turn of the pendulum, causing the 'tick' = 'jar'. [*N*]. 54 **still:** constantly. 59 **posting:** hurrying. 60 **Jack o' the clock:** a figure, generally of metal, which automatically strikes the hours. 62 **holp:** helped. 66 **brooch:** ornament. 'Few dare show they love me in a world where all hate me.' 67–8 There is a play on 'noble', a coin worth 20 groats, and on 'royal' a coin worth 30 groats. [*N*].

The cheapest of us is ten groats too dear.
What art thou? and how comest thou hither, man,
Where no man never comes but that sad dog 70
That brings me food to make misfortune live?

Groom. I was a poor groom of thy stable, king,
When thou wert king; who, travelling towards York,
With much ado at length have gotten leave
To look upon my sometimes royal master's face. 75
O! how it yearn'd my heart when I beheld
In London streets, that coronation day
When Bolingbroke rode on roan Barbary,
That horse that thou so often hast bestrid,
That horse that I so carefully have dress'd. 80

K. Richard. Rode he on Barbary? Tell me, gentle friend,
How went he under him?

Groom. So proudly as if he disdain'd the ground.

K. Richard. So proud that Bolingbroke was on his back!
That jade hath eat bread from my royal hand; 85
This hand hath made him proud with clapping him.
Would he not stumble? Would he not fall down,—
Since pride must have a fall,—and break the neck
Of that proud man that did usurp his back?
Forgiveness, horse! why do I rail on thee, 90
Since thou, created to be aw'd by man,
Wast born to bear? I was not made a horse;
And yet I bear a burden like an ass,
Spur-gall'd and tir'd by jauncing Bolingbroke.

Enter Keeper, *with a dish.*

Keeper. [*To the* Groom.] Fellow, give place; here is no longer stay. 95

70 **sad:** solemn. 75 **sometimes:** sometime, former.
76 **yearn'd:** grieved. 94 **Spur-gall'd:** chafed with the spur.
jauncing: showing one's paces by prancing and careering. 95
here . . . stay: you cannot remain longer here.

K. Richard. If thou love me, 'tis time thou wert away.

Groom. What my tongue dares not, that my heart shall say. [*Exit.*

Keeper. My lord, will't please you to fall to?

K. Richard. Taste of it first, as thou art wont to do. 99

Keeper. My lord, I dare not: Sir Pierce of Exton, who lately came from the king, commands the contrary.

K. Richard. The devil take Henry of Lancaster, and thee!
Patience is stale, and I am weary of it.

[*Strikes the* Keeper.

Keeper. Help, help, help!

Enter EXTON *and* Servants, *armed.*

K. Richard. How now! what means death in this rude assault? 105
Villain, thine own hand yields thy death's instrument.

[*Snatching a weapon and killing one.*

Go thou and fill another room in hell.

[*He kills another: then* EXTON *strikes him down.*

That hand shall burn in never-quenching fire
That staggers thus my person. Exton, thy fierce hand
Hath with the king's blood stain'd the king's own land.
Mount, mount, my soul! thy seat is up on high, 111
Whilst my gross flesh sinks downward, here to die. [*Dies.*

Exton. As full of valour as of royal blood:
Both have I spilt; O! would the deed were good;
For now the devil, that told me I did well, 115
Says that this deed is chronicled in hell.
This dead king to the living king I'll bear.
Take hence the rest and give them burial here. [*Exeunt.*

105 **what means . . . assault**: why does not death come by more gentle means? (He had anticipated poisoning.) 109 **staggers**: causes to stagger, fells.

Scene VI. WINDSOR. AN APARTMENT IN THE CASTLE

Flourish. Enter BOLINGBROKE *and* YORK, *with* Lords *and* Attendants.

Bolingbroke. Kind uncle York, the latest news we hear
Is that the rebels have consum'd with fire
Our town of Cicester in Gloucestershire;
But whether they be ta'en or slain we hear not.

Enter NORTHUMBERLAND.

Welcome, my lord. What is the news? 5
North. First, to thy sacred state wish I all happiness.
The next news is: I have to London sent
The heads of Salisbury, Spencer, Blunt, and Kent.
The manner of their taking may appear
At large discoursed in this paper here. 10
Bolingbroke. We thank thee, gentle Percy, for thy pains,
And to thy worth will add right worthy gains.

Enter FITZWATER.

Fitzwater. My lord, I have from Oxford sent to London
The heads of Brocas and Sir Bennet Seely,
Two of the dangerous consorted traitors 15
That sought at Oxford thy dire overthrow.
Bolingbroke. Thy pains, Fitzwater, shall not be forgot;
Right noble is thy merit, well I wot.

Enter HENRY PERCY, *with the* BISHOP OF CARLISLE.

H. Percy. The grand conspirator, Abbot of Westminster,
With clog of conscience and sour melancholy, 20

10 **At large:** in full. [*N*]. 15 **consorted:** see v. iii. 138.
20 **clog of conscience:** a bad conscience.

Hath yielded up his body to the grave;
But here is Carlisle living, to abide
Thy kingly doom and sentence of his pride.

Bolingbroke. Carlisle, this is your doom:
Choose out some secret place, some reverend room, 25
More than thou hast, and with it joy thy life;
So, as thou livest in peace, die free from strife:
For though mine enemy thou hast ever been,
High sparks of honour in thee have I seen.

Enter EXTON, *with* Attendants *bearing a coffin.*

Exton. Great king, within this coffin I present 30
Thy buried fear: herein all breathless lies
The mightiest of thy greatest enemies,
Richard of Bordeaux, by me hither brought.

Boling. Exton, I thank thee not; for thou hast wrought
A deed of slander with thy fatal hand 35
Upon my head and all this famous land.

Exton. From your own mouth, my lord, did I this deed.

Bolingbroke. They love not poison that do poison need,
Nor do I thee: though I did wish him dead,
I hate the murderer, love him murdered. 40
The guilt of conscience take thou for thy labour,
But neither my good word nor princely favour:
With Cain go wander through the shade of night,
And never show thy head by day nor light.
Lords, I protest, my soul is full of woe, 45

23 **of:** on. 25–6 **some reverend . . . hast:** ambiguous, either (1) some religious house, such as you, playing the politician, have not been frequenting much; or (2) some place where you will be surrounded with more comfort and respect than you have at present. 26 **joy thy life:** enjoy the rest of your life. 35 **of slander:** that will bring slander. 40 **love him murdered:** perhaps deliberately ambiguous; = (1) love the dead man and (2) love the fact that he has been killed.

That blood should sprinkle me to make me grow:
Come, mourn with me for that I do lament,
And put on sullen black incontinent.
I'll make a voyage to the Holy Land,
To wash this blood off from my guilty hand. 50
March sadly after; grace my mournings here,
In weeping after this untimely bier. [*Exeunt.*

48 incontinent: at once.

NOTES

Folio = First Folio of 1623.

References to other plays are made to the one-volume Oxford Shakespeare.

Textual notes and some other more advanced notes are enclosed within brackets, thus [ ].

ACT I. Scene I

The business of the first scene is to introduce some of the characters, make clear the situation, and start the action. The King's dress would indicate his identity, as would his position in the 'chair of state'; note Shakespeare's way of letting the audience know who the others are. The dramatist does well to give a clear statement of the quarrel between Norfolk and Hereford before he heightens the interest by introducing these antagonists. The vague general terms of their preliminary charges against one another (ll. 30–83) provide a good opportunity for rhetoric; the dukes are like lions lashing themselves into a fury. By the time that particular charges are specified, Richard sees that he is personally involved (in the matter of Gloucester's death), and endeavours to compel peace; but the rage of the dukes is now beyond his control. The King's sense of style enables him to withdraw with dignity, if not with honour: 'We were not born to sue, but to command.' The narrower action which fills most of Act I, viz. the quarrel between Hereford and Norfolk, is thus forcibly sketched, and we are left to anticipate future developments in it. The broader theme of the play—the King's failure to control his barons and to rule the land properly—is presented less forcibly at this stage, but is implied in much of the action.

Note Gaunt's withdrawal. He has to appear in the next scene at presumably a different place and time; Shakespeare tries to avoid having him leave the stage to return immediately for the next scene.

1. **Old . . . time-honour'd.** Gaunt was fifty-eight, his brother York fifty-seven. It suits Shakespeare's dramatic purpose to make them appear relics of a more heroic England. Men were considered to enter old age at fifty in Elizabethan times.

2. Both Mowbray and Hereford had been arrested, but the latter was released when Gaunt, York, Aumerle, and Surrey became surety for his appearing to maintain his charge against Mowbray.

15–19. Richard has a poet's power of imagination to appreciate and describe the situation, but lacks a king's power to handle it firmly. The dramatist is rousing anticipation in his audience.

20. A short line metrically.

28. **thou:** used as between relatives. Richard uses 'You' (186) when he is displeased.

43–6. 'The rhymes in the last six lines well express the preconcertedness of Bolingbroke's scheme, so beautifully contrasted with the vehemence and sincere irritation of Mowbray.' (Coleridge.)

43. **aggravate:** used in its proper sense, 'add weight to, increase'.

note. The Roman *nota censoria* was a public disgrace at the hands of the Censor; cf. *Julius Caesar*, IV. iii. 2, 'You have condemn'd and noted Lucius Pella'.

54. Hereford was first cousin to Richard. Cf. l. 59.

78–9. Note Mowbray's subtle appeal to Richard's pride in his kingly power of creating knights.

95. **eighteen years:** since the previous 'treason' of Wat Tyler's Revolt, 1381.

96. **Complotted:** a popular Elizabethan form of *plot*; it stresses the *association* with others.

100 **Duke of Gloucester.** Thomas of Woodstock, Duke of Gloucester, was the seventh son of Edward III, and so Gaunt's brother and Bolingbroke's uncle. His death whilst in custody at Calais, in 1397, while Mowbray was governor there, was thought to be by his nephew Richard's order. Bolingbroke's words are probably directed against the King. It has been said that Gloucester's ghost might well have been added to the list of characters. Why does Shakespeare introduce so often the question of Gloucester's death?

104. **blood . . . Abel's:** cf. *Genesis* iv. 10, 'The voice of thy brother's blood crieth unto me from the ground'.

116. **heir:** i.e. my son. Shakespeare's audience, knowing that Bolingbroke *was* to succeed Richard, would appreciate the irony here and in l. 122.

120. The unusual and stilted diction indicates that Richard is, theatrically, playing a part.

130. In 1395 Mowbray and Aumerle had been sent to propose a marriage between Richard, whose first wife died in 1394, and Isabel, daughter of Charles VI of France. The embassy cost 300,000 marks.

132–4. Mowbray ignores Bolingbroke's second charge, that of 'treason'. His answer to the third throws the blame on Richard; he alludes to his prolonging 'time for the executing of the King's commandment to make the duke secretlie awaie' (Holinshed). The King's next speech shows that he is anxious to avoid further discussion.

153. Choler was supposed to be caused by an excess of bile, one of the 'humours' or essential fluids of the body. Cf. v. v. 10 and note. The parallel from medicine is carried on for five lines. Blood-letting was a kind of cure-all in Shakespeare's day.

156. The King's return to his figure of speech, and his glib 'Forget, forgive', show that he has no depth; such taunts as had passed could *not* be overlooked.

157. [**month**: the First Folio reads *time*. Some think the change was made because spring and autumn were held to be good seasons for blood-letting, and this incident happened in April.]

167–9. 'That' is usually taken to refer to 'name'. It might be taken with 'death' and the line mean 'though you threaten me with death'.

170. **baffled**: 'Originally a punishment of infamy, inflicted on recreant knights, one part of which was hanging them up by the heels' (Nares). The word is very apt here.

186–95. Richard's 'we bid', and his talk of 'lions' come to nothing! Note his less imperious tone to Bolingbroke. The latter does not even argue; he merely refuses.

187. **God.** To comply with the conditions of an act of James I, forbidding profanity, &c., on the stage, the First Folio here and elsewhere (e.g. I. ii. 37, 43), substitutes *Heaven* and makes similar changes.

189. Bolingbroke objects (1) to having to *ask* to be allowed to be honourable, (2) to doing so in Mowbray's presence.

199. **Saint Lambert's day**: September 17.

203. The theory of the Trial by Combat was that the just man won.

204. Mowbray himself was Earl Marshal. Richard appointed the Duke of Surrey as his deputy at Coventry.

ACT I. SCENE II

This scene bridges the necessary interval between the Challenge (April) and the Combat (September), whilst giving a new significance to the latter and rousing our anticipation with regard to it. Hereford becomes, through our pity for the lonely Duchess, the instrument of justice; our hopes are with him. The King's guilt with regard to Gloucester, now made apparent, fills us with a sense of wrong which the evasiveness of Gaunt, with his recourse to the theory of the divine right of kings, does much to aggravate. Gaunt's character is more fully presented here, in preparation for his great speech in Act II, scene i.

The scene is Shakespeare's invention, save for Gaunt's opinion that Richard was guilty.

1. **Woodstock's blood**: see I. i. 113, note.

7. **they**: for Heaven as plural, cf. *Macbeth*, II. i. 4–5: 'There's husbandry in heaven; Their candles are all out.'
hours: a dissyllable.

11–21. In his earlier work Shakespeare often dwells on a metaphor; cf. I. i. 153–7.

15. The Fates or Destinies were imagined as three women, Clotho, Lachesis, and Atropos, who respectively span, measured, and cut the web of each's man's life.

30. The Duchess passes to the more personal appeal.

37–41. Gaunt's reverence for the divinity of kingship, along with that of York (II. iii. 96) and of Carlisle (IV. i. 121–31), makes Richard's attitude throughout the play more comprehensible and less the effect of overweening pride. The crowning of the King was a very solemn ceremony of the Church.

46. **cousin**: used of any degree of relationship save the first; e.g. of nephew, uncle, cousin. Hereford was both her nephew and her brother-in-law.

54. **sometimes**: used interchangeably with 'sometime'.

66. **Plashy**: near Dunmow in Essex. The Duke of Gloucester had a mansion there.

70. [**hear**: the First Quarto has 'cheer', i.e. welcome, entertainment.]

74. 'Thus the Duchess disappears from the action. She is but the voice of Gloucester's blood crying from the ground' (Newbolt).

ACT I. Scene III

The date of this scene is September 17, 1398. Shakespeare follows Holinshed closely, who himself adheres to the procedure of the Trial by Combat.

The scene resolves itself into three parts: (1) the formal pageantry of the preparation for the combat, made more human by Bolingbroke's scorn and Mowbray's quiet pride; (2) the banishment, and oath of non-reconciliation, with Mowbray's hint of his enemy's hidden purpose (204–5), and his own dignity and pathos (154–73) in the face of ingratitude; (3) the parting of Gaunt and his son, which might appear to be given too great prominence here. Shakespeare is aware that Gaunt is shortly to die, and so makes the most of the occasion; but *we* are only aware that Gaunt is old and does not expect to live until his son returns.

The scene marks the crisis of the action begun in scene i; but it is also the beginning of the direct conflict between Richard and Bolingbroke. Note how the King's dilettante nature shows itself in his allowing all the preparations for combat to go forward, before he stops the proceedings; he likes the showy pageant, but he fears almost as much to stop the conflict as to let it go on; he knew that if Bolingbroke were killed, he would be blamed for contriving his death (historically, he was warned that this would happen), whereas if he won, he would be more popular and powerful than ever.

7–45. The dramatist succeeds in making passable verse even out of the fixed and formal procedure of Trial by Combat.

20. If Mowbray were proved guilty of treason, his heirs would rest under attainder.

[**my succeeding issue.** The First Folio reads 'his', which gives an easier meaning; but l. 24 makes it likely that 'my' should be retained.]

55–62. The formal couplets express the cold hypocrisy of the King and the indifference of Bolingbroke: note the change when the Duke turns to others. Richard speaks ambiguously, e.g. 'As thy cause is right' = (only) so far as, &c.

57. **my blood**: the two were full cousins.

68. **The daintiest last.** In Elizabethan times it was a distinctively English practice to end a meal with elaborate confections. Cf. Bacon, 'Let not this Parliament end, like a Dutch feast, in salt-meats; but, like an English feast, in sweet-meats.'

80. **doubly redoubled.** It is usual to allow four syllables to 'redoubled' here, though emphasis is placed more correctly by giving 'doubly' three.

85–96. Contrast the tone of Mowbray's farewell with that of Bolingbroke's. The former sounds more sincere and less boastful.

122. Shakespeare cuts down the 'two long hours' of the withdrawal in Holinshed to a moment's deliberation at the back of the stage. The 'long flourish' means that the King has returned to his 'chair of state' and is ready to make an announcement; hence his 'Draw near'. In the play the decision is made to appear much more sudden and arbitrary than in Holinshed, where, in the interval between what here becomes scene i and scene iii, Richard changes his mind through fear of being accused by the people of aiming at Bolingbroke's death by means of this combat.

127. **aspect:** here, as usual, accented *aspéct.*

129–30. **eagle-winged, sky-aspiring:** cf. I. i. 109, I. iii. 61.

129–38. [Lines 129–33 were omitted in the Folios, as though to get rid of the confusion of 'our peace' frighting 'fair peace' from the land. Perhaps there is some corruption in the text.]

154–73. Mowbray is much more deeply affected than Bolingbroke. The poet is expressing through Mowbray his own patriotic sentiments or those which would please his audience, rather than those likely to be felt by a fourteenth-century nobleman. Mowbray had been Governor of Calais.

159. **forty.** Norfolk's real age is variously calculated at 30–35 years. Elizabethans used the word for a good round number; cf. Puck, 'I'll put a girdle round the earth in forty minutes.'

174. The rebuke comes with an ill grace from one who is often guilty of the same weakness, i.e. self-pity.

181. There is no historical authority for Richard's releasing the banished dukes from their duty of allegiance to him. In any case it is probable that their banishment would automatically do so.

185–6. **Nor never:** the double negative is common in Shakespeare. It gives emphasis here to Richard's administering of a vow the terms of which he cannot enforce.

189–90. The tautological ending of a speech which reads like some legal formula.

196. **sepulchre:** accented *sepúlchre*, the noun here being accented as the verb always is in Shakespeare.

204–5. Mowbray is aware of Bolingbroke's designs; so was the King, cf. I. iv. 20–2. 'Richard's treachery to Mowbray was a blunder as well as a crime' (Chambers). The hint here given is dramatically effective in rousing anticipation. It also stirs fear in Richard, and he hastens to make a futile attempt at conciliation. The remission actually took place some weeks later, and because of popular indignation.

213–15. Bolingbroke's almost contemptuous words imply that kingly power is too great to be wielded so capriciously.

226–32. The 'hoary majesty' of Gaunt's years and grief looms up to rebuke the shallow optimism of Richard; it is as though the curtain had been rung up on the drama of human existence, dwarfing the play and players into insignificance.

234. Shakespeare did not invent this. The Bishop of Carlisle says, in Holinshed, 'the Duke was banished from the realme by King Richard and his counsel, and by the judgement of hys owne father'.

248. Exeunt, &c. As in *A Midsummer Night's Dream* (I. i. 127). Shakespeare, aided by the conditions on the Elizabethan stage, saves the trouble of making a new scene by having some of the characters somewhat unnaturally remain behind.

249. It seems very strange that Aumerle should take his leave here, when the next scene indicates that he went some distance with Hereford. One would expect also a separate *Exit* for him, here. The different characters of Gaunt and his son are clearly revealed in the parting which fills the remainder of the scene.

258–64. Dialogue in alternate lines, or *stichomythia*, appears frequently in the writers of Greek and Latin tragedy. Shakespeare adopts it chiefly in his earlier works. Cf. *Richard III*, IV. iv.

258. Is 'thy' emphatic? Gaunt knows he is ill.

261. Cf. *As You Like It*, III. ii. 326–51.

263–70. With this passage, which expresses Bolingbroke's matter-of-fact mind, contrast Richard's successful 'imaginings', V. v. 1 ff.

262. **travel**: there may be a pun on 'travail'.

268–93. [Omitted in the First Folio; perhaps a stage cut in the copy used for Folio.]

271–4. The apprentice had to serve a period of years as a learner or pupil; he then obtained his freedom, was called a journeyman, and could work for hire (possibly by the day, Fr. *journée*). Bolingbroke puns on '*journey*-man'.

291. **measure:** commonly used by Shakespeare of any dance, but here in its technical sense of a slow and stately one; cf. *Much Ado About Nothing*, II. i. 80, 'as a measure, full of state and ancientry'.

302–3. The idea seems to be that these imaginings which Gaunt advises Bolingbroke to indulge in would merely aggravate the pain of the exile, without being able to cure it.

306–9. Note the significant contrast between Bolingbroke's farewell to England and Richard's greeting to her upon his return from Ireland (III. ii). Richard conceives his country as his 'child', to whom he 'does favours with his royal hands', and of whom he expects single-minded loyalty in his service. Bolingbroke conceives it as his 'mother' and 'nurse', 'to whom he owes what he is, and who will be his boast and glory in exile' (Herford).

ACT I. Scene IV

There is some confusion as to the date of this scene: the King and his courtiers are still discussing Bolingbroke's departure, which was begun in scene iii, yet the scene ends with the report that Gaunt is dying, which really took place six months after Bolingbroke's departure (February 3, 1399). Shakespeare is again dependent on Holinshed for material. The scene makes clear the attitude of the people to Bolingbroke, and the King's dislike of him and insight into his purposes; it shows Richard's dependence on favourites and his indifference to the goodwill and welfare of his subjects, high and low, so long as he can indulge his own caprice.

1. **We did observe:** spoken to Bagot and Green. Cf. l. 23 below.

3–4. Aumerle's pun on 'high' sets the tone of contempt for what follows. The King's question (l. 5) is ironical.

16–19. Cf. IV. i. 15–17 for the sentiment.

20–22. These lines are deliberately ambiguous. They may mean, 'whether he shall be allowed to come back when his time is up' or 'whether he won't come back to supplant me rather than see his friends'. Richard means to try to keep him out of the country. He now realizes that the sentence of banishment may have been a mistake; it has roused popular indignation in Bolingbroke's favour.

23. **Bushy.** Sir John Bushy, Speaker of the House of Commons. Holinshed says he was very ambitious and flattered Richard with terms more suited 'to the divine majestie of God, than to any earthlie potentate'.

24. Cf. *1 Henry IV*, III. ii. 50, where Bolingbroke, now King, tells his son how he won popular favour:

> And then I stole all courtesy from heaven,
> And dress'd myself in such humility
> That I did pluck allegiance from men's hearts,
> Loud shouts and salutations from their mouths,
> Even in the presence of the crowned king.

28. **craftsmen . . . craft:** note the pun. Richard's attitude to the common people is one of scorn.

35. Roger, Earl of March, heir-presumptive to the throne, was killed in Ireland in July 1398; this made Richard's expedition to Ireland necessary. The King's scornful attitude to Bolingbroke's hopes is full of irony for the audience, who know what is to happen.

45. For a sum down (£7,000 per month) Richard sold to Bushy, Bagot, Green, and the Earl of Wiltshire the right to collect for themselves all revenues due to him from his land, taxes, &c.

58. **Ely House:** the palace of the Bishop of Ely in Holborn. Cf. *Richard III*, III. iv. 33, where the King asks for some strawberries from the palace garden.

61. Richard's callous speech prepares us for his conduct in the next scene.

ACT II. Scene I

This scene follows I. iv almost immediately in time. Gaunt died in February, 1399; Bolingbroke landed in July of the same year. Yet (1) in I. iv Bolingbroke is spoken of as just leaving England, and (2) he is here spoken of as having returned! In the interval he has been to France, has had his marriage to the French king's cousin 'stayed' by Richard's interference, and is returning to England ostensibly to assert his claim to his estates (II. iii. 129 ff.) which are *only now* being denied to him! On the stage this confusion is not felt, and the 'telescoping' of events suits the dramatist's purpose.

In ll. 1–146 the matter is of Shakespeare's invention. The fervent idealism of this passage provides at once the background against which Richard's reckless injustice is to be set, and the standard by which it is to be judged. We are put in the proper frame of mind for censuring Richard's conduct in seizing Lancaster's estates (147–223), and for welcoming the turn of the tide in the news of Bolingbroke's landing (224–300).

The fine poetry of Gaunt's great speech needs no comment; 'it gives a very echo to the seat' where patriotism is throned. Coleridge remarks that it contains every motive and inducement to patriotism. The poetry of the later passages is somewhat spoiled by excessive word-play. Note that Gaunt now charges Richard directly with Gloucester's murder; but we are made to feel that the King's destiny is settled; there is no changing or repentance in him; he must 'dree his weird'.

7–16. Note the use of rhyme, a mark of early work, especially the quatrain, ll. 9–12. Even in the later plays Shakespeare retains couplets for sententious moralizing.

18. [The First Quarto reads, *of whose taste the wise are found*; the Second has *state* for *taste*; the later Quartos and the Folios, *of his state: then there are found*. Collier's conjecture of *fond* for *found* is very frequently adopted.]

21–3. Writers of Shakespeare's time frequently complain of the popular imitation of things Italian, particularly by young men of fashion. In the actual time of Richard French influence was dominant.

23. **imitation**: five syllables.

28. **wit**: in the wider sense of power of understanding.
regard: either (1) view, opinion, or (2) that which is looked upon favourably, to which 'regard' is had.

34–9. Gaunt seeks confirmation of his opinion, after the manner of the old, in 'wise saws'. Note the figurative nature of his speech. In his later poetry Shakespeare was much less careful to see that each figure of speech was completely worked out.

35. Study the onomatopoeic effect of this line.

40–55. These lines, save line 50, are quoted in *England's Parnassus*, an anthology published in 1600; they are attributed there to 'M. Dr.', i.e. Michael Drayton. 'The spirit of patriotic reminiscence', says Coleridge, 'is the all-permeating soul of this noble work', and that patriotism finds here its highest expression.

49. **less happier**: coined for emphasis on the analogy of Shakespeare's double comparatives like 'more happier'.

55. The Jews were considered to reject Christianity out of mere stubbornness.

56. 'The Son of Man came to give His life a ransom for many.' Matthew xx. 28.

73–83. Coleridge has put up the best defence for the quibbling in Gaunt's speech; see *Lectures on Shakespeare*, pp. 151–2 (Bohn ed.). See line 85 for Gaunt's own explanation. This drama has many other plays on words.

89. Gaunt's words here, as at l. 93, are ambiguous. He may be alluding to the adage *de mortuis nil nisi bonum*; more probably his meaning is made clear in l. 91.

100–3. i.e. 'Your head is full of the words of your flatterers, and, small as the head is, yet the whole country is involved in the results of their flattery.'
verge probably contains allusion to the technical 'verge' or 'compass of the king's court, or the jurisdiction of the lord steward of the royal household, which extended for 12 miles round' (Rolfe).

103. **waste.** 'A law term for the destruction of houses, wood, or other produce of land, done by the tenant to the prejudice of the freehold' (Clark and Wright).

104–7. By the Commons' petition Richard was declared heir to the throne in the last year of Edward III's reign.

114. There is probably a quibble on 'bond'; cf. l. 64.

118–19. Cf. III. ii. 75–9, IV. i. 265–7. Richard's handsome, sensitive face showed his feelings all too readily. It is like him to make poetry out of the circumstance!

126. **pelican.** According to the popular bird-lore of the Middle Ages, this bird revived its young with its own blood. Cf. *King Lear*, III. iv. 74, where Goneril and Regan are called 'pelican daughters'.

133. **crooked:** suggesting Time with his sickle in l. 134.

137. **Convey.** It is highly improbable that one so sick as Gaunt is would be moved; but to remove him effects greater economy of time than to have his guests depart and reassemble elsewhere for what follows. What difficulty in Elizabethan stage management is indicated by the direction 'borne out by his attendants'?

141–4. York is as weak as his words are ambiguous. He means to say (ll. 143–4) that Gaunt loves Richard as much as he loves his son; but he leaves the way open for Richard's misinterpretation, that Gaunt loves him as little as Bolingbroke loves him.

146. **all be as it is.** This expression may be taken as implying a fatalistic acceptance or 'fey-ness' on Richard's part, and as expressing his inability to do anything to save himself.

157. 'Rugs' were coarse frieze cloaks, made in Ireland. The poet Spenser in 1596 says the Irish wore 'long glibbes, which is a thick curled bush of hair, hanging down over their eyes, and monstrously disguising them'.

158. Probably alluding to the tradition that St. Patrick expelled the snakes.

164. Historians tell us York loved hunting and his own ease, and disliked public business. Coleridge finds in him 'religious loyalty struggling with a deep grief and indignation at the king's follies'.

168–9. **prevention . . . marriage.** Charles VI of France received the exiled Bolingbroke well and would have given him his cousin in marriage, but Richard sent the Earl of Salisbury to break off the match.

178. Richard was thirty-two. His father was the Black Prince.

200 ff. York's judgement was fully justified. Richard's action gave Bolingbroke an excuse to return with right on his side, it made the barons fear similar treatment, and it destroyed all confidence in Richard's good faith, since Bolingbroke had had his promise to be allowed legally to 'sue his livery'. 'As a special favour Bolingbroke had received (by letters-patent) the privilege of appointing substitutes (attorneys-general) who were authorized to claim possession in his name of any bequest or other property falling to him' (Herford). Richard got his parliamentary council to annul the privilege six weeks after Gaunt's death.

204–5. **sue . . . homage.** Under feudal tenure, lands held from the King lapsed to him on the death of the tenant; the heir had to apply for them (Fr. *livrée*, delivery) by proving he was of age, paying a year's profits (*firmer seisin*), and offering homage.

211. The dramatist gets York out of the way of the conspirators. Note how the use of the rhyme emphasizes the warning.

218. Wiltshire (previously Sir William le Scrope) was treasurer of England. He was beheaded at Bristol (II. ii. 134–5).

218. Actually three months elapsed at this point.

222. A line rich in irony, in view of what York has just been saying!

225–300. Practically a separate scene, and the beginning of the plot or series of activities which is to be used to balance Richard's doings. If Shakespeare had been concerned to make the seizure of his estate Bolingbroke's real excuse for return, he would have made an interval at this point, to allow of the news reaching France, before telling us that Bolingbroke is *already* in arms.

248–9. Richard levied a poll-tax of fourpence in 1381, which roused the Commons, and in 1399 fined seventeen shires for having aided the Lords Appellant, Gloucester, Arundel, and Warwick, in an 'ancient quarrel' with him in 1387.

[The repetition and the lame metre make it very likely that the text is corrupt. The subject was one on which Elizabeth was touchy, and some words may have been cut out or altered.]

253–6. Richard's policy was one of peace with France. In 1396 he married Charles VI's daughter and concluded a twenty-eight years truce. Many in England opposed him, and blamed him for giving up what in fact he had no right to retain, e.g. Brest and Cherbourg.

264. **sing**: cf. *Tempest*, II. ii. 19. 'Another storm is brewing; I hear it sing i' the wind.'

281–2. [Probably a line is lost here with the sense 'The son of Richard, Earl of Arundel', and 'that late broke' does not refer to Cobham, unless Shakespeare's haste led him to make a slip. For Holinshed says that the son of Richard, Earl of Arundel, escaped from Exeter's house; and since the Archbishop's brother was that Richard, he must have been mentioned with his son, in the lost line or lines.]

282. **Archbishop late.** When the Earl of Arundel was executed for treason in 1397, his brother the Archbishop was banished for complicity in the plot.

289–90. Holinshed says Bolingbroke delayed until he should find out how far the people would favour him. He also gives two accounts of Bolingbroke's landing, one in which he arrives with only fifteen men, the other as Shakespeare gives it here. It is fitting that Northumberland should be given the more encouraging, but the dramatist uses the other at will. Cf. *1 Henry IV*, IV. iii. 56–63.

296. **Ravenspurgh**: or Ravenspurn, near Spurn Head, on the Humber; most of it was washed away by high tides, in the fourteenth and early fifteenth centuries.

ACT II. SCENE II

The date of the scene is early July, 1399. The matter in lines 1–40 is the invention of Shakespeare; for the rest, he used Holinshed.

The first forty lines are similar in effect to scene ii of Act I; they increase and prolong the foreboding produced by Gaunt's prophecies in the previous scene, and secure for Richard, through the pathos of the Queen's helplessness, a measure of that sympathy which he had entirely lost.

Note the way in which the scene is managed—the cumulative effect of the entries of Green, York, and servant, each with bad news, as though to substantiate the Queen's foreboding, and the final touch of the scattering of the favourites—like rats deserting a sinking ship. Even they, however, scarcely expect to escape.

6. **I know no cause:** cf. *Merchant of Venice*, I. i. 1, 'In sooth I know not why I am so sad'.

18–27. **perspectives:** 'At Gerards Bromley, there are the pictures of Henry the great of France and his Queen, both upon the same indented board, which if beheld directly, you only perceive a confused piece of work; but if obliquely, on one side you see the king's and on the other the queen's picture' (Plot, *Natural History of Staffordshire*, quoted by Staunton).

'Perspectives, looked at directly (rightly), reveal only confusion; looked at from an angle, reveal definite shapes. You look on the King's departure from a particular angle, and see it multiplied into many shapes of grief; if you looked at it directly, there would be only the one thing to sorrow for.' Unfortunately for Bushy, the parallel does not quite hold, since there *is* one genuine 'shape of grief'; but even it, looked at 'directly', would not be visible as it really is.

34–40. i.e. 'It is anything but an imaginary trouble. An imaginary trouble is always (*still*) based on some previous trouble; mine is not of that nature. It springs from no cause, and yet is genuine (*something*); or some real person has the affliction of which I bear the sorrow, and I shall know what the cause of my sorrow is only in the future, when the possession of the affliction reverts to me. But there is no telling what it is just now.' Shakespeare dare not make her forebodings regarding Richard definite; to do so would spoil the effect of what is to follow.

57. **[rest of the revolted faction.** So the Quartos except the First, and the First Folio: the First Quarto has 'rest revolted faction'. Cf.

As You Like It, II. vii. 39, 'as dry as the remainder biscuit'; *Henry VIII*, II. iv. 46–7, 'one The wisest prince that'. The reading of the First Quarto suits the metre.]

58–61. Worcester, Northumberland's brother, broke his white staff, the sign of his office as Steward of the Royal Household, in the presence of the King's servants—but this was really *after* Richard's return from Ireland.

86. Historically, Aumerle had gone with Richard to Ireland from the start.

97. 'The Duchess of Gloucester died in October, not in July; at Barking, not at Plashy; of grief for her son's, not her husband's death' (Newbolt). But it is convenient for the dramatist to have 'the accumulated woe' here.

98–121. In this whole passage the metre is so slipshod as to suggest corruption in the text; some critics have even suggested it should be in prose. It certainly expresses vividly York's distraction, caused by '(1) the practical difficulties—want of money and means; (2) the fact that he is equally near of kin to both parties; (3) the sense that the whole situation is but a Nemesis upon Richard's guilt' (Herford).

102. Gloucester was smothered between two beds, not executed.

103. **no posts**: for six weeks, at the time of Bolingbroke's landing, the weather was so rough that no ship could cross to Ireland. Cf. l. 123.

105. **Come, sister,—cousin.** York is thinking of the dead Duchess.

136. According to Holinshed, Wiltshire, Bushy, and Green flee together to Bristol.

144. It does not occur to the favourites to help York.

ACT II. Scene III

This scene, showing the rising tide of Bolingbroke's fortunes, is an effective contrast to the previous one. In structure it is curiously similar, consisting of a series of entries with cumulative effect until even the King's deputy, York, finds himself in the usurper's power. Bolingbroke was popular in London, and knew that he would be independent of the nobles when he reached that city; meanwhile he professes humility to them, desiring only to gain possession of his estates and to make the King govern more justly. It would seem from Shakespeare's presentation of the unctuous flattery of

Northumberland that he already had in mind the man who failed his own son at need in *1 Henry IV*. Reference should be made to I. iii. 239 ff.; IV. iii. 52 ff.; V. i. 30 ff. of that play for the later attitude of the Percies to Bolingbroke.

The scene is at Berkeley, July 27, 1399.

4. Shakespeare knew the Cotswolds which lie between Stratford-on-Avon and Berkeley, which is north of Bristol.

7. **delectable:** accent on first and third syllables.

33. **over:** one syllable, 'o'er'.

41–4. It suits Shakespeare's purpose to make Percy here and throughout *1 Henry IV* much younger than he really was, so as later to provide in him a contrast to Prince Hal. Percy was at this time 35 years of age—two years or so older than Richard and Bolingbroke.

70. **my answer is—to Lancaster.** Malone inserted the dash, making the line mean 'Your message is to Lancaster', rather than 'I answer only to the name of Lancaster'.

80. **self-born:** only the later Folios omit the 'e' in 'self-borne'. The unsettled Elizabethan spelling does not enable us to determine whether the meaning is, (1) 'born within ourselves', and so, 'civil' (cf. civil war), or, as is more probable, (2) 'borne', i.e. carried, 'in your own cause, not in the king's'.

87. **Grace me no grace:** a common mode of expressing contemptuous disagreement. Cf. *Romeo and Juliet*, III. v. 153: 'Thank me no thankings, nor proud me no prouds.'

101–3. Historians have found no record of this incident. Shakespeare may have read Nestor's boast in the *Iliad*, vii. 157; Hall's translation appeared in 1581.

107–8. York's reply gives the word 'condition' its ordinary meaning of 'state'; i.e. 'It is as bad as it can be.'

117–18. Bolingbroke deftly turns York's recollections of Gaunt to his own purpose.

163. York is quietly annexed by the alert Bolingbroke.

165. **Bagot:** cf. II. ii. 141 and III. ii. 122.

ACT II. Scene IV

Richard sent Salisbury to Wales to assemble troops, meaning to follow himself in six days. This scene tells what happened to the 40,000 men (according to Holinshed) that Salisbury got together. The latter's words are full of pathos. Clearly the King is to be thrown upon the resources of his own character. The scene is near Conway; the time, July 28, 1399.

1. **ten days**: fourteen, in Holinshed; probably changed for the sake of the metre.

8. It is only in the *second* edition of Holinshed (1586) that 'old baie trees withered'. The withering of the laurel, the tree emblematic of victory, was held to be a bad omen. The portent is mentioned by Holinshed in another connexion, but Shakespeare converts it to his purpose.

15. An old belief. Cf. *Julius Caesar*, II. ii. 31: 'The heavens themselves blaze forth the death of princes.'

17. Storms delayed Richard's return from Ireland so much that a rumour arose that he was dead.

19–20. Cf. III. iii. 178.

21. 'Richard's badge was the sun obscured by clouds' (Newbolt); cf. III. ii. 36–53 and III. iii. 62–7.

24. For the audience the passage is full of ominous anticipation.

ACT III. Scene I

Bolingbroke's kingly dignity in his treatment of the favourites is a foretaste of his manner as a ruler; he carries out his limited aims to the letter. The fall of the favourites heralds that of the King; already the usurping duke assumes authority over life and death. One senses in Bolingbroke the power that succeeds; perhaps his care for the Queen is intended by Shakespeare to soften the impression we receive of his character.

3. For transitive use cf. *Pericles*, v. iii. 38, 'When we with tears parted Pentapolis'; see Abbott's *Shakespearean Grammar*, p. 198.

11–15. The charge has no historical foundation; it is a reminiscence of Marlowe's *Edward II*. The Queen was only ten years old, and the previous Queen had been dead five years. But it suits Shakespeare's purpose to make Bolingbroke chivalrous. Cf. l. 37.

20. Cf. *Romeo and Juliet*, I. i. 138: 'Adding to clouds more clouds with his deep sighs.'

25. Steevens quotes Ferne's *Blazon of Heraldry* (1585), that 'the arms, &c., of traitors may be defaced and removed, wheresoever they are fixed, or set'.

34. **injustice:** Bolingbroke has already gone beyond his rights in assuming the power of life and death.

36. **your house:** Langley, see III. iv.

43. **[To fight . . . complices.** Some think this line spurious, since it breaks the usual couplet-tag, and is historically inaccurate. Bolingbroke's first campaign against Glendower took place in autumn, 1400. But Holinshed says Glendower served Richard at Flint Castle, and Shakespeare may have assumed he was the 'Welsh Captain'; cf. II. iv. Holinshed speaks of 'the said Owen and his *complices*'.]

ACT III. SCENE II

Shakespeare ignores Holinshed's account of how the King was decoyed out of Conway and carried off to Flint by Northumberland. The place is probably Harlech, Merionethshire, and the date July 29, 1399.

The scene should be compared in structure with II. ii and II. iii. It is conducted in the same way by a series of entries and accumulation of announcements, with intervening lyrical outbursts by the King, whose character is now developed in great detail. It is more effective dramatically than those mentioned, since it reaches a more dramatic climax, and since the announcements are of importance only as they stimulate some new outburst from the King. Study in detail the ebb and flow of hope and despair in Richard, and contrast his address to England with Gaunt's great speech. Pater's 'pathos of kingship' (see Critical Extracts) is particularly evident in the latter part of the scene.

1. **Barkloughly:** Holinshed gives the name as *Barclowlie*, which is almost certainly a printer's or copyist's error for *Hertlow* or *Hertlowi*, i.e. Harlech.

4 ff. There is an excellent contrast between Bolingbroke's love of England and Richard's. Try to analyse the difference. Both would endear them to an Elizabethan audience.

14. It was thought that spiders could suck poison from flowers.

14–22. 'Richard, in the crisis of action, creates about him a fairyland full of wise and faithful beasts, and the armed troops wait inactive on the shore while their leader invokes the aid of nettles and spiders' (Herford).

33. Aumerle bluntly expresses the moral of the Bishop's veiled words.

38. Cf. II. iv. 21, note.

41–61. It is possible to excel as a poet and fail as a king!

67 ff. This dates the scene as one day later than II. iv.

70. **twelve:** Holinshed says forty.

75–6. Cf. II. i. 118.

75–81. Notice the quatrain followed by a couplet. Such rhymes only occur in early plays of Shakespeare.

83 ff. 'A sort of wordy courage which only serves to betray more clearly his internal impotence' (Coleridge).

93–103. Richard's mind seems to find satisfaction only in an extreme position which allows him a striking pose. Before he knows how much he has lost, he is already picturing himself as having lost all and as losing it with a magnificent gesture of renunciation.

114. Shakespeare may have had the boy-actors in mind.

122. **Bagot.** Richard inquires about *four* favourites, but at l. 132 speaks of *three*, and at l. 141 Aumerle ignores Bagot. At II. ii. 140, Bagot speaks of fleeing to Ireland. Bolingbroke thought he was in Bristol Castle, II. iii. 165. He reappears as a prisoner in London, IV. i. Shakespeare remembers his pawns when it suits him!

127–8. For similar dramatic irony cf. *Macbeth,* IV. iii. 176–9.

144. Richard shows the same readiness as at l. 93 to sink into the extreme (but effectively poetic) position before he has heard all. Scroop's heavier news is thus held in suspense; the releasing of it brings about Richard's decision to go to Flint Castle, and so ends the scene.

For the tenor of the speech that follows, cf. *3 Henry VI*, II. v, *Henry V*, IV. i. 250 ff.

153–4. **small model . . . bones:** somewhat ambiguous. Most probably it means 'our bodies', or rather, 'the flesh of our bodies', which are 'models' or copies of the earth in that they are 'dust of the ground'; of them, and of death, we cannot be deprived. Some think the reference is to the rounded mould on a grave, the 'six foot of earth'. Johnson comments on l. 154: 'A metaphor, not of the most sublime kind, taken from a *pie*.'

156. **sad stories . . . kings.** Shakespeare probably had in mind such popular medieval and Elizabethan collections of sad tales as Boccaccio's *De Casibus Virorum Illustrium*, Lydgate's *Falls of Princes*, and Sackville's *Mirror for Magistrates*, in which Richard's own story appears.

161. This image may have been suggested to Shakespeare by the seventh print in the *Imagines Mortis* where there is a king represented sitting on his throne, sword in hand, with courtiers round him, while from his crown rises a grinning skeleton.

164. **scene:** it is natural for Shakespeare the actor to draw images from the stage. Cf. *Macbeth*, v. v. 24: 'Life's but a walking shadow, a poor player', &c.

166. 'Self' is an adjective, almost = selfish. 'Conceit' has changed its meaning, for in Eliz. English it meant 'thought' or 'fancy', not 'pride'.

168. **humour'd thus:** very ambiguous; it may mean (1) 'when he (the antic) has exercised his "humour" or whim of puffing the king up with pride', or (2) 'while the king is in this "humour of conceit"', or (3) '*after* the king has been indulged in this way for a "breath"'.

169. The 'pin' represents the small cause which may destroy the fortunes of a human body.

175–6. Some words may have dropped out, making the metre defective.

183–5. 'If you fear to fight, you will certainly be killed; no worse can happen by resisting. He who dies fighting may *either* kill his enemy, the cause of his death, *or* triumph over death (since he conquers the fear of it); whereas to die in fear of death is to admit his power over you.' As often, the glimpse we catch of the meaning when the poetry is read quickly is hard to reduce to plain terms.

ACT III. Scene III

Omitting as he does the decoying of Richard out of Conway, Shakespeare is compelled to make other changes; for Northumberland in the chronicle was already (August 18, 1399) in possession of Flint Castle, and of the King; next day Bolingbroke arrived there. Aumerle had already joined the usurper and was not in Flint.

The preliminary skirmish between York and Northumberland suggests the question—Who is king, the man with the name or the man with the power? Thereafter the capacity of the stage is taxed by the display of Bolingbroke's troops, the appearance of the King and others on the balcony, and the effort to preserve dignified ceremonial in limited space. More than any one there the King sees the significance of his fall and its consequence, sees the symbolism and poetry of the occasion, and less than any one is he able to provide a remedy. Even while he yields, he flatters himself that he *could* play the part of the defiant non-yielder! Note how quickly Shakespeare, having brought Richard down from the balcony, brings the scene to an end, with Bolingbroke's quiet exercise of superior power whilst he professes to be a subject still.

12–14. There is a play upon words in 'to be brief with': in l. 12 it means 'to use few words' (and so omit titles); in l. 13 it means 'to be curt with, to give short shrift to'. Also on 'take the head', which means (1) 'behave without regard to authority' (as of a horse), and (2) 'omit the title'.

21. According to Holinshed, Northumberland had already taken Flint Castle, had gone to Conway, whither Richard had fled, and had induced him to return to Flint. Richard was already in all but name a prisoner; but it would have spoiled a dramatic scene to have had him appear so.

32. Coleridge finds in what follows 'the fine struggle of a haughty sense of power and ambition in Bolingbroke with the necessity for dissimulation'.

47. **fair**: may refer to 'land' as well as to 'King Richard'.

52. [**tatter'd.** The first and second Quartos read 'totter'd'. There was frequent confusion between the two words in Elizabethan English.]

58. **yielding.** There is no yielding in Bolingbroke. He must be taken to mean 'apparently yielding, pliant'. l. 60 shows it is the possession of England he aims at.

94. The line is obscure and *might* mean 'to see what war will leave him'.

95–6. Prophetic reference to the evil effects of usurpation are frequent in the play. Cf. iv. i. 136.

126. **commends:** cf. iii. i. 38. At this point Northumberland withdraws—without ceremony. Richard wonders if he has hit the proper pose!

136. Hurt pride and baffled incompetence mingle strangely to produce Richard's regret.

140 ff. For the manner of the speech, cf. iii. ii. 93 ff. Note the effective use of the impersonal 'king', and compare Caesar's use of 'Caesar'. Richard shows no strength or skill: 'By holding Bolingbroke to his word, he could have placed him in the dilemma of having either to disband his forces or seize the king by violence' (Herford).

147–53. The accumulation of parallel single-line clauses was a feature of Shakespeare's more rhetorical speeches at this time. Cf. *King John*, iii. iv. 29–33.

149. The luxuriousness of the Court was notorious. Richard had 'a coat of gold and stone' valued at 3,000 marks.

153–8. The very ecstasy of sentimental renunciation.

159. **buried once:** for the absolute construction, cf. 'humour'd thus', iii. ii. 168.

162. **lodge:** beat down; cf. *Macbeth*, iv. i. 55, 'The bladed corn be lodg'd and trees blown down.'

168. **There lies:** *hic jacet*, the opening of the epitaph. Singular verbs with plural subjects are fairly frequent in Shakespeare, especially after 'there', 'here'. Cf. ll. 184–5.

176. Richard has been speaking from the balcony above the rear portion of the stage.

178. **Phaethon:** son of Helios, the Sun-God. He obtained his father's permission to drive the chariot of the sun for one day, but, unable to manage the horses, he nearly set the earth on fire; whereupon Zeus slew him with a thunderbolt. He typifies youthful presumption. Richard's figure is apt.

187–8. Appropriate instruction to the actors as to how to behave.

192. **Me rather had.** This impersonal construction (cf. 'methinks') is the result of the coalescing of the personal 'I had rather' (cf. 'I had as lief', V. ii. 49) and of the impersonal 'me were lever', i.e. it would be more pleasing to me.

204. Both were born in 1366, and so were thirty-three years old. Richard throughout is made to seem young; cf. II. i. 69–70.

ACT III. SCENE IV

This beautiful scene—'an islet of repose' Coleridge called it—is laid in York's garden at Langley, in late September, 1399. As in the other scenes of the play where women are present, the pathos is intense. The scene is a kind of allegory of what has happened—'a summary and parable of the action of the whole play', it has been called—and is intended, whilst it shows the Queen's grief, to reveal also what the people feel. It anticipates the deposition and directs our minds forward to the King's fate. Note the device of overhearing and the consequent irony.

Stage Direction. *Langley*. Editors infer from l. 70, with II. ii. 116 and III. i. 36, that York had the Queen in keeping at his palace at Langley, near St. Albans.

11. [**joy:** Rowe's necessary emendation for 'grief', found in all the Quartos and Folios.]

27–8. A dramatic anticipation; cf. II. ii. 41–end.

29. **apricocks:** the usual Elizabethan spelling. The fruit had not been introduced into England in the fourteenth century.

34–9. The gardener's words about his duties have all a further application for the audience to affairs of state at the moment. ll. 38–9 must suggest Richard's favourites who are unprofitable to the country, as is made clear in l. 50.

47. **caterpillars:** an echo of II. iii. 166, as l. 43 is of II. i. 47.

58–9. The words 'skin', 'over proud', and 'blood' are introduced to keep the metaphorical application to men clearly in our minds.

72. **press'd to death.** Accused persons who refused to plead and remained obstinately silent were formerly punished by having increasingly heavy weights laid upon their chests. The Queen finds having to listen in silence to the gardener such a punishment.

73. **old Adam's likeness.** The gardener is so called since Adam was the first gardener (cf. Genesis ii. 15: God 'put him into the garden to

dress it'); and the mention of Adam suggests the use of 'Eve' and 'serpent' for temptation in l. 75.

78. **thou, thou:** used in contempt. Cf. *Twelfth Night*, III. ii. 50: 'If thou thou'st him some thrice, it shall not be amiss.'

79. The Queen believes in prognostications, as we saw in II. ii. 9–12.

86. 'The early physicists believed that some things had a property of positive levity or lightness, instead of gravity' (Chambers).

105–6. The flower 'rue' was a symbol of repentance and was often mingled with the holy water; hence 'herb of grace', 'herbygrass'. But the name was confused with 'ruth' = pity, regret, and Shakespeare plays on the association here. Cf. *Hamlet*, IV. v. 180–1, when Ophelia says to Laertes, 'There's rue for you . . . we may call it herb of grace o' Sundays.'

ACT IV. Scene I

For the material of Aumerle's arraignment, Carlisle's protest, and the Abbot's conspiracy, Shakespeare is indebted to Holinshed; the deposition scene is largely the dramatist's own, though Froissart relates that Richard, in his royal robes, handed over the crown and sceptre to Bolingbroke in presence of the nobles. Shakespeare telescopes the events of October 16 (when Bagot accused Aumerle), October 18 (when Fitzwater and others challenged Aumerle, Surrey challenged Fitzwater, &c.), and October 22 (when the Commons asked that judgement against Richard be recorded and published, and Carlisle protested), and links them to those of September 30. The conspiracy was begun on December 17.

This scene is the climax or crisis of the play; and yet it consists rather of a number of exciting incidents than of one impressive situation; for Richard is in reality no longer king. The quarrel regarding Gloucester's death serves to remind us of Richard's guilt, whilst exhibiting the turbulence of the nobles and Bolingbroke's power. Carlisle's protest is a reminder of the persistence of the opposition and affects us in the way that courageous loyalty always does; the audience would be moved by his prophecy, since they knew it was fulfilled. The actual deposition scene depends greatly upon the acting for its effectiveness; it is so easy to convert it into the chastisement of the clever eccentric fop of a boy by the sturdy bully. Looked at more largely, it is the spectacle of life correcting its errors; the powers of the poet and of the actor, in themselves, are not qualifications for the occupant of a throne; and the removal of the impediment to just government by the grim power of Bolingbroke constitutes an impressive, if painful, spectacle, as though life crushed something beautiful and attractive out of its way.

Westminster Hall. Richard had just rebuilt Westminster Hall, 1397–9. The first time Parliament met in it, they deposed him!

1. **Bagot:** cf. note to III. ii. 122.

10. Cf. I. i. 100, where Bolingbroke accuses Mowbray of this.

14. **that very time:** but Gloucester was dead before Bolingbroke was exiled.

21. **fair stars:** 'that particular conjunction of stars at my nativity which made me of high rank'. By the code of chivalry, Aumerle might refuse combat to one so far beneath him in birth as Bagot.

24. **attainder:** originally = 'loss of civil rights upon conviction for treason'; then, through confusion with 'taint', = 'disgrace of an accusation successfully maintained against one'.

33. 'Sympathy' was formerly used of any agreement or conformity, not only that of feeling.

40. **rapier.** It does not trouble Shakespeare that the rapier was introduced into England, along with other Italian weapons and duelling terms, only in his own day.

44. Shakespeare had no evidence that Percy was present at this Parliament, though he was probably there. Fitzwater's challenge, Holinshed says, was issued two days after Bagot's charge. In both cases, the poet suits his convenience.

52. He throws his gage down as Percy has done. The Folios omit ll. 52–9.

65. **boy:** Surrey speaks in contempt; Fitzwater was thirty-one.

67. **vengeance and revenge.** The tautology, for once, gives emphasis. Such combinations are frequent, e.g. 'joy and felicity', but generally the two words are derived from different languages.

84. **this.** Holinshed tells us he borrowed 'another hood' to throw down.

86. It has been suggested that Bolingbroke already knew of Norfolk's death, and hence could appear to be generous; but this is hard to prove. Certainly he is doing his best to conciliate the nobles by a show of impartiality.

91–100. Holinshed does not mention Norfolk's crusading activities. Stow's *Annals* (1580) records that he died on returning from Jerusalem.

107–12. York welcomes the abdication with easy complaisance. Can you reconcile this with his previous attitude? Note the effective contrast with Carlisle, who would not speak of the King by divine right as 'plume-pluck'd'.

109. **Adopts thee heir:** fulfilling that which is rejected in I. i. 116 and I. iv. 35–6.

114–49. The first part of Carlisle's speech, to l. 135, is from Holinshed; in it he maintains Richard could not justly be tried *in absentia*. The latter part, in which he prophesies civil war, is Shakespeare's invention.

116. Verity notes 'that the part which the Church really took in Richard's deposition, and which Shakespeare saw in Holinshed, is entirely omitted in the deposition-scene that follows. It could not have been introduced after Carlisle's protest. The inconsistency would have been too confusing'.

136–44. Shakespeare is thinking of the Wars of the Roses. This part of the speech links the play strongly to *1 Henry IV*.

141. ['The words *kin* and *kind* are not always clearly distinguished in Shakespeare. *Kin* (OE. *cynn*) originally meant "kind", "race", "tribe"; *kind* (OE. *ge-cynde*), "nature". The latter sense was, after Chaucer, more and more expressed by the word "nature"; and *kind* tended to become confused with *kin*, a confusion fostered by the word *kind*-red (OE. *cyn-red*)' (Herford).]

144. **Golgotha:** see Matthew xxvii. 33, 'a place called Golgotha, that is, a place of a skull.'

145. Cf. Matthew xii. 25, 'And every city or house divided against itself shall not stand.'

150–3. [Holinshed says the Earl Marshal, i.e. the Earl of Westmoreland, arrested Carlisle. Northumberland had been Marshal in Edward III's reign, and was Lord High Constable under Richard. Holinshed also says Carlisle was sent to the Abbey of St. Albans. More accurately, he was sent to the Tower and later put into the care of the Abbot of Westminster, as here.]

154–318. [These lines appeared for the first time in the Third Quarto of 1608. See Introduction.]

173. **priest and clerk:** when the priest prayed the parish clerk led the responses.

175. Richard is still convinced he is king 'in God's sight'.

186–9. The comparison is only applicable at some points, since Bolingbroke is by no means empty.

190. Admirably blunt for the contrast Shakespeare wishes to draw.

195–7. **Your cares . . . won.** Richard is quibbling on 'care', = (1) sorrow, (2) responsibility. 'The addition to your troubles does not involve a proportionate decrease in mine. My sorrow is for loss of responsibility, for the removal of that which occasioned me anxiety; what you have to lament is increase of anxiety through your new "charge", i.e. the kingship.' ll. 198–9 repeat l. 195.

201–2. **Ay, no . . . to thee.** Wretched quibbling on 'I' and 'ay' (printed 'I' in the old editions). 'Ay—no, not "ay", for if I say "ay" it reduces me to nothing; and yet not "no", since I must yield.' He will not say positively he agrees to resign, but he also will not say he doesn't!

205–10. For the style of rhetoric, cf. III. iii. 147–53.

210. [**duty's rites.** The Oxford text interprets the Quartos' 'duties rites' as 'duteous rights', which would bear the same sense. The First Folio reads "dutious Oathes'.]

212. **revenues:** scan *revénues,* and contrast I. iv. 46; cf. *recórd,* l. 230, and *récord* I. i. 30.

232–3. 'Wouldst' and 'shouldst' would be reversed in modern usage.

239–42. They try to escape responsibility by pretending to pity the king, as Pilate did by washing his hands. See Matthew xvii. 24, 26, and cf. ll. 170–1.

254. A reminiscence of Marlowe's *Edward II,* v. i. 112–13 (another abdication scene):

'*Winchester*. My lord. . . .
Edward II. Call me not lud . . . out of my sight.'

l. 262 recalls Marlowe's *Faustus,* v. iv, 'O soul, be changed to little water-drops, And fall into the ocean, ne'er be found.'

255–7. Richard's baptismal name of John was changed later because it was supposed to be unlucky; after his deposition he was often referred to as John of Bordeaux (his birthplace) or John of London. His enemies also spread the report that he was really the son of a canon of Bordeaux, not of the Black Prince.

276. Opinion differs greatly as to the merit of the 'mirror' scene. See the Critical Extracts.

281–3. Cf. Faustus's speech, when Mephistophilis conjures up a vision of Helen of Troy (*Faustus*, v. iii):

> 'Was this the face that launch'd a thousand ships,
> And burnt the topless towers of Ilium ?'

Holinshed tells us 10,000 people had 'meat and drink' daily from Richard.

293–9. Richard interprets Bolingbroke as saying that such acts as the breaking of the mirror are only the outward show, the 'shadow', of deep internal grief, only the 'external manners of laments'. But Bolingbroke probably meant that Richard's grief was as insubstantial as the reflection of his face in the mirror.

305. **'Fair cousin!'** Like a drowning man, Richard clutches at straws. His despair resembles that of a clever weak boy beaten by a bully.

317–19. **convey . . . nimbly:** 'convey' and 'conveyance', from being used of secret arrangement, acquired a bad sense and became euphemistic slang for 'steal', 'stealing'. Cf. *Merry Wives*, I. iii. 28–30:

> '*Nym*. The good humour is to steal at a minim's rest.
> *Pistol*. "Convey," the wise it call.'

[There may be a pun in 'nimbly'. *Nim*, originally = 'take', was in common use in that sense until the fifteenth century. 'During the sixteenth there are few traces of it, but immediately after 1600 it reappears . . . as a slang or colloquial word in the sense of "to steal".' (*O.E.D.*)]

324–34. Shakespeare loses no time in rousing our interest in a new part of the plot. He seems to forget that Carlisle was under arrest for 'capital treason', and would not be left unattended. But he effects an economy in time by having the conspirators left behind.

ACT V. Scene I

Richard and his Queen actually parted in April (II. ii. 1–4) for the last time; this scene, supposed to take place immediately after Act IV, is wholly invented. The Queen did not return to France until June 1401. Richard was removed from the Tower to Leeds Castle, in Kent, and finally, in late autumn, 1399, to Pontefract (Pomfret), in Yorkshire.

The scene is a relief from the harsher business of politics. The Queen has much of Richard's talent for poetic figure, and it is interesting to watch them wing their flight, like a pair of butterflies, among the more tender emotions. In places, Richard's spirit seems more 'finely touched' than anywhere else in the play.

2. **Julius Cæsar's ill-erected tower.** Legend held that the tower of London was built by Julius Caesar, though it was really erected by William the Conqueror to overawe London. Cf. *Richard III*, III. i. 68–79, where the tradition is discussed.

8. **rose:** cf. *1 Henry IV*, I. iii. 175, where Richard is called 'that sweet lovely rose'.

11–15. Strong feeling moves the Queen, as it does her husband, to a highly wrought vein of fancy. The lines are spoken of the king, who is now 'the mere ground-plan or foundations of a city once great, the outline (map) of power, rather than the reality it represents, the grave that holds what is left of a king. Why should triumph take up her lodging in a common ale-house (i.e. Bolingbroke), when she might live in a beauteous inn (i.e. Richard) where at present grief resides?'

Troy. There was indeed a legend that London was founded by Trojan refugees and called Troynovant; but Troy stands here simply for a symbol of past grandeur.

20. **sworn brother.** An allusion to the custom among knights of vowing to share each other's fortunes; they were then *fratres iurati*, sworn brothers.

24–5. Resignation and repentance appeal much more to the poetical Richard than resistance. Cf. III. ii. 93–103, III. iii. 147–52. His lack of spirit provokes the Queen, although she has no more hope than he has.

29–31. Again a reminiscence of Marlowe. Cf. *Edward II*, V. i. 11–14:

> 'But when the imperial lion's flesh is gored,
> He rends and tears it with his wrathful paw,
> And, highly scorning that the lowly earth
> Should drink his blood, mounts up to the air.'

34. **lion:** recalling, with pathetic irony, Richard's words at I. i. 174, 'lions make leopards tame'.

48. 'The poet should have ended his speech with line 45, and have spared his childish prattle about the fire' (Johnson).

55–69. A strong link with *1 & 2 Henry IV*; in the latter play (III. i. 70–8) Bolingbroke quotes part of this speech. Shakespeare is prophesying after the event; the audience knew how fully Richard's words were fulfilled.

80. **Hallowmas.** All Saints' Day, November 1. Before the change in the calendar this would be November 12, nearer to the shortest day than now.

101. Richard is conscious that they have been overdoing somewhat the role of parting lovers.

ACT V. Scene II

The excitement of the main conflict of the play, that between Richard and Bolingbroke, being now practically at an end, Shakespeare fills in the always-difficult part of the action between crisis and catastrophe with matter from the Abbot of Westminster's plot. But first, in York's description, he carries the contrast between King and usurper even into the details of their reception by the people. Shakespeare is here inventing, for the two did not enter London on the same day; but the narrative is none the less vivid. What follows is based on Holinshed, save that the Duchess was not Aumerle's mother. The action is conducted dramatically, with much vigour, and a degree of exaggeration, both in this scene and the next, that approaches the grotesque; apparently the dramatist felt the need of stir and bustle to keep his play alive. The conspiracy makes more inevitable the fate of Richard; it is very useful in other ways to the dramatist.

The place is probably intended to be Langley, not London, otherwise the Duchess would scarcely be asking for the description York gives; the time is January 4, 1400.

6. Most of the detail of this description derives from the poet's imagination. Richard was detached from Bolingbroke's triumphal procession a few miles from London and taken to Westminster by a different route, whilst his captor went to St. Paul's.

12–17. Tapestries or arras, ornamented with mottoes or with figures which had mottoed labels issuing from their mouths, were in common use as wall-hangings and would seem to have been taken down and hung out of the windows on festive occasions. But the words 'with painted imagery' do not prove this, since they may still be a metaphorical description of the people hanging out of the windows.

18. Cf. i. iv. 24–36.

23–6. An experience with which the actor Shakespeare was probably familiar. It does not trouble the poet that there were no 'theatres' in England for more than 150 years after this.

30. **sacred:** cf. ll. 37–40. A clear and rational understanding of its basis does not seem to be necessary to York's loyalty—or disloyalty.

38. The idea is that of Dante's line, 'In la sua volontade è nostra pace', i.e. 'in His will is our peace'.

41. **my son.** Aumerle was her step-son, and not her only one (cf. l. 90), and she was much younger than Shakespeare makes her appear to be. Without these alterations this scene and the next would lose much of their force.

The Dukes of Aumerle, Exeter, and Surrey were reduced to the status of Earls on November 3, 1399.

44–5. It is important that the audience should know this; otherwise York's conduct towards an adult son would seem rather highhanded.

48. **nor . . . care not:** the double negative is emphatic; cf. IV. i. 255, and V. v. 39.

56–7. **seal . . . writing.** The seal would be attached to the parchment on which the letter was written. Actually it was one sent to Aumerle from Huntingdon, Kent, and Salisbury, warning him to be ready; they were already assembled with 8,000 men at Kingston, at which place, not Oxford, their plot was to be carried into effect.

92–3. The Duchess was Richard II's niece and her desire to save one at least of the conspirators might thus be explained. Cf. l. 41, note.

97. **A dozen.** Holinshed names nine; six signed the bond.

98. Each signed the bond and each received a copy with all the signatures. Cf. Holinshed's 'indenture sexpartite'.

111. **his horse.** York's horse would be ready by this time.

115. Hall's Chronicle tells us that Aumerle rode post to Windsor, 'whiche his father being an olde man could not do'.

ACT V. Scene III

This is really a continuation of scene ii, save that Bolingbroke's talk of his son is introduced to mark the interval and the transition to Windsor. In addition, that talk helps to link the play with *1 Henry IV*, and presents Bolingbroke's faith in his son, in spite of appearances, in contrast to York's conduct as a father. The scene is conducted, as before, with a good deal of melodramatic vigour, touched with comic relief. Bolingbroke shows his strength both in his attitude to his son and in his treatment of York and Aumerle.

1. The son was at this time 12 years old; see note to II. iii. 41–4.

10. [**While:** Pope's emendation of 'which', the reading of all Quartos and Folios. The construction is obviously loose. 'Which' might be taken as referring to the companions or to their conduct as described.]

67–73. York is clearly prompted by self-interest in this unnatural degree of loyalty to his new master.

79–80. Bolingbroke's tone here and in l. 81 heralds comedy. The allusion is to the title of a ballad, 'King Cophetua and the Beggar Maid', formerly called 'A Song of a Beggar and a King'. Cf. Tennyson's *Beggar Maid.*

118. A common thought in Shakespeare (cf. *Merchant of Venice,* IV. i. 196–7) and in contemporary drama, both at home and abroad.

122. **sett'st . . . word:** cf. V. v. 13–14. Shakespeare is probably thinking of those who set one text from Scripture against another and produce misinterpretations.

124. **chopping:** the meaning is far from clear. Suggestions are: (1) mincing, affected; (2) jerky; (3) changing (cf. 'chop and change'), so that *pardon* can be converted into 'excuse me', i.e. a refusal of a pardon. The audience would relish the epithet, whether they understood it or not!

128. 'Pierce' rhymes with 'rehearse'; cf. Falstaff's quibble on Percy, *1 Henry IV,* V. iii. 58, 'If Percy be alive, I'll pierce him'.

137. **brother-in-law and the abbot:** the Earl of Huntingdon, late Duke of Exeter—who proposed the tourney—and the Abbot of Westminster. Pronounce *broth'r* and *th' abbot.*

145. **true.** Aumerle, then Duke of York, fell fighting for Henry at Agincourt; see *Henry V,* IV. vi. 3–32.

ACT V. SCENE IV

The Folio and the Quartos seem not to regard this as a separate scene; the Quartos have the direction, '*Manet Sir Pierce Exton*'. The material is from Holinshed. For a more dramatic management of the same *motif* see *King John,* III. iii. 60 ff. Aumerle's conspiracy, however, must have shown Bolingbroke that he was not safe as long as Richard was alive.

1. **Didst thou . . . spake:** for the construction cf. III. iii. 61, 'mark King Richard how he looks'. It is difficult to be quite clear as to when Exton is supposed to have heard the words spoken. Holinshed says Exton heard these words whilst waiting on the King at table.

ACT V. SCENE V

For the details of Richard's death, Shakespeare is indebted to Holinshed; the monologue and the incident of the groom he invented; unless, indeed, the latter were inspired by Froissart's story of Richard's devoted greyhound Mathe, which at Flint castle for the first time fawned on some one else—Bolingbroke.

The monologue (finely relieved and stimulated by music) shows Richard still the poet, the devotee of fancy; and as when king he tried to drive his subjects by his own caprice, so as poet he tries to compel his fancy to invent unnatural images. His interview with the groom shows him in a good light; obviously he can inspire affection. In the end, like Hamlet, he is driven out of his day-dreams into action, but his is the courage of a desperate rather than of a resolute man.

9. According to ancient belief, man was *microcosmos* (= little world), a model in miniature of the great world, *macrocosmos*; hence the astrological belief in the correspondence of the movements of the planets and stars with changes in man's fortunes.

10. **humours.** The four elements, air, water, fire, and earth, were supposed to appear in man as the four essential fluids or humours of the body, blood, phlegm, choler, and bile or melancholy, respectively; according as any one of these predominated, a person was sanguine, phlegmatic, choleric, or melancholy. From the changing nature of human dispositions, 'humour' came to mean 'mood', 'caprice', 'eccentricity'. Cf. I. i. 153.

13–14. [The Folios, here and at V. iii. 122, have *faith* instead of 'word'.]

15–17. The texts are Matthew xix. 14 and xix. 24. In the latter, the 'eye of a needle' is sometimes explained as 'a narrow town-gate'.

[The Folio reads 'needle', but the Quartos have 'small needle' which assumes the common alternative form 'neeld'; cf. M.ND. III. 2. 204.]

20–1. **flinty:** cf. V. i. 3. One part of the Tower was of flint.

31. For the theatrical metaphor, cf. V. ii. 23.

[All the old texts save the First Quarto read *prison* for 'person'.]

33. The 'treason' presumably consists of unthroning a king—even in imagination.

51–8. Difficult lines. Time is measured by (1) the internal movements of the watch, (2) the result of these shown by the hand on the dial (the 'outward watch'), (3) the sound of the bell striking the hours. So Richard's *thoughts* are the internal movements marking the minutes; his thoughts result in sighs, which collect until they show outwardly in *tears*, and these bring his finger into play, which thus becomes the pointer or hand of the dial; his *groans* mark the hours.

57–8. 'Tears' and 'times' correspond; so that 'times' must mean the larger divisions of the hour, other than minutes, marked by the hand. Some take 'times' = the figures on the clock-face.

61. So music is played as Lear recovers (*King Lear*, IV. vii) and by David to Saul when a fit of melancholy has seized him (1 Samuel xvi).

66. Shakespeare may be alluding to the fact that brooches were going out of fashion (as adherence to Richard was).

67. **noble peer:** spoken in bitter mockery of the groom's mode of address.

67–8. 'The cheapest of us' is usually taken to mean the 'noble', and Richard to say that he and the groom are so come down in the world as to be worth only half their face value; but he *may* mean that the ten groats difference between the 'royal' and the 'noble' is obliterated; he and the groom are on a level, hence the play on 'peer'.

100–1. There is probably corruption in the text, reducing it to prose, since the Keeper has already spoken in verse.

ACT V. Scene VI

Shakespeare ends his play with another scene built round a series of announcements reaching a climax. All Bolingbroke's enemies are accounted for; and the advent of the last, which should mark the climax of his triumph, almost converts the play into tragedy. The ending is ominous; it remains to see whether the wheel will 'come full circle'.

The scene is not historical, but is probably supposed to take place at Windsor. Note that *1 Henry IV* opens with Bolingbroke about to make his pilgrimage.

3. **Cicester:** Cirencester, in Gloucestershire. The Quartos and Folios have 'Ciceter', which represents the local pronunciation.

6. **sacred.** Northumberland adopts York's attitude when it suits him.

9–10. The winding-up of the play must be done swiftly; hence the device of the 'paper'.

19–21. Most authorities hold that the Abbot of Westminster introduced into the play was William of Colchester, who, however, is generally believed to have lived till 1420.

30 ff. Cf. *King John*, IV. ii. 203 ff.

31. **buried fear:** cf. 'living fear', V. iv. 2.

35. [**slander:** all the texts save the First Quarto read 'slaughter'.]

49–50. Bolingbroke repeats this wish at the opening of *1 Henry IV.*

SELECT LITERARY CRITICISM

KINGSHIP IN SHAKESPEARE

True, on the whole, to fact, it is another side of kingship which he has made prominent in his English histories. The irony of kingship—average human nature, flung with a wonderfully pathetic effect into the vortex of great events; tragedy of every-day quality heightened in degree only by the conspicuous scene which does but make those who play their parts there conspicuously unfortunate; the utterance of common humanity straight from the heart, but refined like other common things for kingly uses by Shakespeare's unfailing eloquence: such, unconsciously for the most part, though palpably enough to the careful reader, is the conception under which Shakespeare has arranged the lights and shadows of the story of the English kings, emphasizing merely the light and shadow inherent in it, and keeping very close to the original authorities, not simply in the general outline of these dramatic histories but sometimes in their very expression. . . . No! Shakespeare's kings are not, nor are meant to be, great men: rather, little or quite ordinary humanity, thrust upon greatness, with these pathetic results, the natural self-pity of the weak heightened in them into irresistible appeal to others as the net result of their royal prerogative. One after another, they seem to lie composed in Shakespeare's embalming pages, with just that touch of nature about them, making the whole world akin, which has infused into their tombs at Westminster a rare poetic grace.

(PATER: *Shakespeare's English Kings.*)

THE CHARACTER OF RICHARD

In this play, the character of Richard, carefully and slowly wrought, dominates the whole, makes the events and makes the catastrophe. It is the play. The character of Bolingbroke is quite secondary. Its outlines are drawn, but they are only partly filled up. What he is meant to be is more seen in his opposition to Richard than in himself. He is the strong man against the background of whose character the weakness of Richard stands out clear.

(BROOKE: *On Ten Plays of Shakespeare*)

The amiable part of Richard's character is brought full upon us by his queen's few words:

> . . . So sweet a guest
> As my sweet Richard ;—

and Shakespeare has carefully shown in him an intense love of his country, well knowing how that feeling would, in a purely historic drama, redeem him in the hearts of the audience. Yet even in this love there is something feminine and personal:

> Dear earth, I do salute thee with my hand, . . .

With this is combined a constant overflow of emotions from a total incapability of controlling them, and thence a waste of that energy, which should have been reserved for actions, in the passion and effort of mere resolves and menaces. The consequence is moral exhaustion, and rapid alternations of unmanly despair and ungrounded hope—every feeling being abandoned for its direct opposite upon the pressure of external accident. And yet, when Richard's inward weakness appears to seek refuge in his despair, and his exhaustion counterfeits repose, the old habit of kingliness, the effect of flatterers from his infancy, is ever and anon producing in him a sort of wordy courage which only serves to betray more clearly his internal impotence.

(COLERIDGE: *Lectures on Shakespeare.*)

Richard, to whom all things are unreal, has a fine feeling for 'situations'. Without true kingly strength or dignity, he has a fine feeling for the royal situation. Without any making real to himself what God or what death is, he can put himself, if need be, in the appropriate attitude towards God and towards death. Instead of comprehending things as they are, and achieving heroic deeds, he satiates his heart with the grace, the tenderness, the beauty, or the pathos of situations. Life is to Richard a show, a succession of images; and to put himself into accord with the aesthetic requirements of his position is Richard's first necessity. He is equal to playing any part gracefully which he is called upon by circumstances to enact. But when he has exhausted the aesthetic satisfaction to be derived from the situations of his life, he is left with nothing further to do. He is an amateur in living; not an artist.

(DOWDEN: *Shakespeare, His Mind and Art.*)

Richard II is among the Histories what *Romeo and Juliet* is among the Tragedies, an almost purely lyrical drama, swift and simple. Richard is possessed by the sentiment of royalty, moved by a poet's delight in its glitter and pomp, and quick to recognize the pathos of its insecurity. There is nothing that we feel in contemplating his tragic fall which is not taught us by himself. Our pity for him, our sense of the cruelty of fate, are but a reflection of his own moving and subtle poetry. Weakness there is in him, but it hardly endears him the less; it is akin to the weakness of Hamlet and of Falstaff, who cannot long concentrate their minds on a narrow practical problem; cannot refuse themselves that sudden appeal to universal considerations which is called philosophy or humour. Like them, Richard juggles with thought and action: he is a creature of impulse, but when his impulse is foiled, he lightly discounts it at once by considering it in relation to the stars and the great scheme of things. What is failure, in a world where all men are mortal? Sometimes the beating of his own heart rouses him to fitful activity:

Proud Bolingbroke, I come
To change blows with thee for our day of doom.

Then again he relapses into the fatalistic mood of thought, which he beautifies with humility:

Strives Bolingbroke to be as great as we?
Greater he shall not be: if he serve God
We'll serve him too, and be his fellow so.

(RALEIGH: *Shakespeare.*)

King Richard is of a type very interesting to Shakespeare. He is wilful, complex, passionate, with a beauty almost childish, and a love of pleasure that makes him greedy of all gay, light, glittering things. He loves the music that does not trouble with passion and the thought not touched with the world. He loves that kind of false, delicate beauty which is made in societies where life is too easy. There is much that is beautiful in him. He has all the charm of those whom the world calls the worthless. His love is as a woman, as beautiful and unreal as himself. He fails because, like other rare things, he is not common. The world cares little for the rare and the interesting. The world calls for the rough and common virtue that guides a plough in a furrow, and sergeantly chaffs by the camp fires. The soul that suffers more than other souls is little regarded here. The tragedy of the sensitive soul, always acute, becomes terrible when that soul is made king here by one of the accidents of life. . . . He is not fitted for kingship, but life has made him a king. Life, quite as much as temperament, is to blame for his tragedy.

(MASEFIELD: *William Shakespeare.*)

The next play was probably *Richard II* which is again a play in which one figure fills the whole stage. The king is everything in it; but the everything is as unlike that of *Richard III* as it could well be. There we have the picture of cunning and violence hurrying furiously from murder to suicide: here we have weakness and folly passing on their primrose path from pleasure, vanity, fine phrases and incompetence to failure, desertion, and death. Richard III acts; Richard II only suffers. Of action he is incapable: for action requires will, and he has nothing but desire. From the first he displays the fickle irresolution always to be observed in men of mere desire and sentiment. Principles of action, good or bad, of this world or another, he has none; he tosses irresolute on a sea of fancies with neither god nor devil at his helm. The very first scene shows the stuff of which he is made. He will have Mowbray and Bolingbroke accept a reconciliation; but when they will not he at once submits, and all the satisfaction his kingship gets is the self-flattering words with which he graces his defeat:

We were not born to sue, but to command.

And so all through the play. Again and again he changes at a word. He orders the duel and stops it at the very last moment.

He sentences Bolingbroke to ten years' exile and commutes it to six at a look, without even a spoken word, from Gaunt. In the third Act his conduct, or rather his succession of moods, for he does nothing, is the very picture of irresolution. He has hardly finished posturing with the comforting assurance that the very earth will turn her stones into soldiers at the call of the king, making lovely speeches to convince himself that

> Not all the water in the rough rude sea
> Can wash the balm from an anointed king,

when at a stroke of bad news he is at once sure that all is lost and advises all to leave him. But that mood instantly passes at a reminder of his kingship:

> Is not the king's name twenty thousand names?

And then that, too, is hardly uttered before it is changed to

> The worst is death, and death will have his day.

And, even after that, there is one more brief recovery, immediately followed by:

> Beshrew thee, cousin, which didst lead me forth
> Of that sweet way I was in to despair!

There is the dominant note of the theme: the 'sweet way' to despair. For men of his type all is sensation: when he is confronted with the demand for a decision his answer is 'Ay, no: no, ay', as in the abdication scene; he and such as he neither wish to act nor can. What they ask for and must have is, for their minds a succession of dreams, for their bodies a continuous luxury of sensations; and their love of passiveness is such that they will make a luxury of pain and shame and death itself. The end is Nirvana, always the ultimately welcome haven of the senses which have deluded themselves with the pleasant fancy that they are the whole and not a subordinate part of man:

> whate'er I be,
> Nor I nor any man that but man is
> With nothing shall be pleased, till he be eased
> With being nothing.

And yet there are people, two at least of whom one would be sorry to call fools, who will have it that this poor creature was a kind of favourite child in the eyes of that rare unity of wisdom and strength which we know by the name of William Shakespeare! They tell us that Richard II failed 'a little because he lacked some qualities that were doubtless common among his scullions, but more because he had certain qualities that are uncommon in all ages'; and that he was certainly 'greater in the divine Hierarchies' than Henry V, who is 'the one commonplace man' in the Histories. Fools such critics are, whatever their distinction, at least in one dangerous way of folly. They cannot endure the humility of seeing with all men's eyes or telling a truth that has been told before. And so they must needs have Richard II as the 'vessel of porcelain' and Henry V as the 'vessel of clay'. For their own choice Mr. Yeats and Mr. Masefield are free. Only they must not father it upon Shakespeare. No man has ever known the theatre better than he; and if he had meant us to admire Richard and despise Henry we should most assuredly not have escaped doing it; but there is no audience from his day to ours which has not instantly and instinctively worshipped Henry and pitied Richard. One might as well be asked to believe that Shakespeare liked Iago better than the less intellectual Othello, or meant us to prefer Macbeth, who makes such wonderful speeches, far finer even than Richard's, and can do things, too, which Richard cannot, to the plain virtues of Banquo or Macduff. No: Shakespeare knew always what he was doing; and it is not by mistake or incompetence that he has made it clear to us that the feeling he had meant us to have for his Richard is one not of admiration but of pity.

The mistake of course comes just from that. Because Shakespeare was so profoundly and so widely human he could not but love all or very nearly all his creatures, though pity is the only form love can take with some of them. But it is the merest delusion to fancy, because he has been inside them all and knows how they appear to themselves and can give each of them a voice to state his case, that he accepts their statement or sees them as they see themselves. That is the madness which has made some people fancy he meant Shylock to be a sympathetic figure; Shylock, almost whose first word, a word spoken only to his own ears, is

> If I can catch him once upon the hip,
> I will feed fat the ancient grudge I bear him.

To Shakespeare Shylock is not the monster of crime, nor Richard II the monster of folly, which he might be to other people. Neither is for him incredible or inexplicable: he has in his hands the thread which unravels the mystery. But that does not mean that he does not judge them and make us do so.

(BAILEY: *The Continuity of Letters.*)

THE CHARACTER OF BOLINGBROKE

BOLINGBROKE utters few words in the play of *Richard II*; yet we feel that from the first the chief force centres in him. He possesses every element of power except those which are spontaneous and unconscious. He is dauntless, but his courage is under the control of his judgement; it never becomes a glorious martial rage like that of the Greek Achilles, or like that of the English Henry, Bolingbroke's son. He is ambitious, but his ambition is not an inordinate desire to wreak his will upon the world, and expend a fiery energy like that of Richard III; it is an ambition which aims at definite ends, and can be held in reserve until these seem attainable. He is studious to obtain the good graces of nobles and of people, and he succeeds because, wedded to his end, he does not become impatient of the means; but he is wholly lacking in genius of the heart; and therefore he obtains the love of no man. He is indeed formidable; his enemies describe England as

> A bleeding land,
> Gasping for life under great Bolingbroke;

and he is aware of his strength; but there is in his nature no fund of incalculable strength of which he cannot be aware. All his faculties are well-organized, and help one another; he is embarrassed by no throng of conflicting desires or sympathies. He is resolved to win the throne, and has no personal hostility to the king to divide or waste his energies; only a little of contempt. In the deposition scene he gives as little pain as may be to Richard; he controls and checks Northumberland, who irritates and excites the king by requiring him to read the articles of his accusation. Because Bolingbroke is strong, he is not cruel. He decides when to augment his power by clemency, and when by severity. Aumerle he can pardon, who will live to fight and fall gallantly for Henry's son at Agincourt. He can dismiss to a dignified retreat the Bishop, who, loyal to the hereditary principle, had pleaded against Henry's title to the throne. But Bushy, Green, and such like caterpillars of the Commonwealth, Henry has sworn to weed and pluck away. And when he pardons Aumerle he sternly decrees to death his own brother-in-law. . . . There is nothing infinite in the character of Henry, but his is a strong finite character.

(DOWDEN: *Shakespeare, His Mind and Art.*)

THE CHARACTER OF YORK

THERE is scarcely anything in Shakespeare in its degree, more admirably drawn than York's character; his religious loyalty struggling with a deep grief and indignation at the king's follies; his adherence to his word and faith, once given, in spite of all, even the most natural, feelings. You see in him the weakness of old age, and the overwhelmingness of circumstances, for a time surmounting his sense of duty—the junction of both exhibited in his boldness in words and feebleness in immediate act; and then again his effort to retrieve himself in abstract loyalty, even at the heavy price of the loss of his son.

(COLERIDGE: *Lectures on Shakespeare.*)

York is self-contradictory, unprincipled, vacillating, composite, and incoherent, but in no sense obscure. He in the first place upbraids the King with his faults, then accepts at his hands an office of the highest confidence, then betrays the King's trust, while he at the same time overwhelms the rebel Bolingbroke with reproaches, then admires the King's greatness in his fall, then hastens his dethronement, and finally, in virtuous indignation over Aumerle's plots against the new king, rushes to him to assure him of his fidelity and to clamour for the blood of his own son. There lies at the root of this conception a profound political bitterness and an early-acquired experience.

(BRANDES: *William Shakespeare.*)

THE MIRROR SCENE

SHAKESPEARE has evidently spent so much trouble over this scene that he has overdone his work. He has introduced that spectacular scene with the mirror which is quite unnecessary, which sins against the 'Not too much', and which, worst of all, not only lowers our pity for Richard because it exhibits his theatrical folly in public, but also degrades the character of Bolingbroke below the level it keeps in the rest of the play. In permitting this antic of Richard, Bolingbroke lays him open to a cruel mockery which his terrible sorrow neither deserves nor ought to have. I wonder Shakespeare's exquisite delicacy towards human nature could have permitted it. Nor is it the only stain on the scene. Shakespeare should have felt that Northumberland's demand that the king, round whom the compassion of all gentle folk should gather, must read out, and sign the record of, all his crimes and follies, was a brutal demand. It is also needless for the dramatic action, and, if it be done to increase the pity for Richard which ought to preside over the scene, is a clumsy way of doing this. There is pity enough. It needs no false heightening.

(BROOKE: *On Ten Plays of Shakespeare.*)

The mirror-scene at the deposition—which, like the sleep-walking scene in *Macbeth*, seems to have been wholly of Shakespeare's invention—is a wonderful summary and parable of the action of the play.

(RALEIGH: *Shakespeare.*)

THE PARTING OF RICHARD AND HIS QUEEN

(RICHARD) is purged of his weakness. He is purged of his selfishness. He is purged of his blindness. He is purged of his insolentia. He speaks no longer with a flux of words. All he says is brief and clear. He sees with equal steadiness the past, the present, and the future. His love is no longer a feeble sentiment. The parting with his Queen is marked by strength and self-control deeply set in love, and with the wisdom of death in every word. He knows he is the victim of Fate, and he knows why—

> Join not with grief, fair woman, do not so,
> To make my end too sudden: learn, good soul,
> To think our former state a happy dream;
> From which awak'd, the truth of what we are
> Shows us but this. I am sworn brother, sweet,
> To grim Necessity, and he and I
> Will keep a league till death.

Can any words, any temper, be more unlike his previous words and temper? . . . All that was weak and foolish has passed away, but his lovingness is deepened by the change. His parting words are lovely with tenderness and sweet rememberance.

(BROOKE: *On Ten Plays of Shakespeare.*)

THE POETRY OF THE PLAY

ONE gracious prerogative, certainly, Shakespeare's English kings possess: they are a very eloquent company, and Richard is the most sweet-tongued of them all. In no other play perhaps is there such a flush of those gay, fresh, variegated flowers of speech—colour and figure, not lightly attached to, but fused into, the very phrase itself—which Shakespeare cannot help dispensing to his characters, as in this 'play of the Deposing of King Richard the Second', an exquisite poet if he is nothing else, from first to last, in light and gloom alike, able to see all things poetically, to give a poetic turn to his conduct of them, and refreshing with his golden language the tritest aspects of that ironic contrast between the pretensions of a king and the actual necessities of his destiny. What a garden of words! With him, blank verse, infinitely graceful, deliberate, musical in inflexion, becomes indeed a true 'verse royal', that rhyming lapse, which to the Shakespearian ear, at least in youth, came as the last touch of refinement on it, being here doubly appropriate. His eloquence blends with that fatal beauty, of which he was so frankly aware, so amiable to his friends, to his wife, of the effects of which on the people his enemies were so much afraid, on which Shakespeare himself dwells so attentively as the 'royal blood' comes and goes in the face with his rapid changes of temper.

(PATER: *Shakespeare's English Kings.*)

It is difficult to condemn Richard without taking sides against poetry. He has a delicate and prolific fancy, which flowers into many dream-shapes in the prison; a wide and true imagination, which expresses itself in his great speech on the monarchy of Death; and a deep discernment of tragic issues, which gives thrilling effect to his bitterest outcry:

Though some of you, with Pilate, wash your hands,
Showing an outward pity, yet you Pilates
Have here delivered me to my sour cross,
And water cannot wash away your sin.

(RALEIGH: *Shakespeare.*)

APPENDIX I

THE LIFE OF WILLIAM SHAKESPEARE

(condensed from Sir Edmund Chambers's *William Shakespeare*)

WILLIAM SHAKESPEARE was born of middle-class parents at Stratford-on-Avon, a provincial market town of some importance, at an uncertain date between April 24, 1563, and April 23, 1564. His parents were natives of Warwickshire. His father, John Shakespeare, whose principal business was that of glover, rose high in civic life, becoming alderman in 1565 and bailiff in 1568, but later fell on evil days. His mother was Mary Arden. Shakespeare was educated at King Edward VI's Grammar School, Stratford, where he must have learnt a fair amount of Latin, if little or no Greek. He married in 1582 Anne Hathaway, and his first child, Susanna, was baptized in May 1583, to be followed in February 1585 by twins, Hamnet and Judith. Susanna's daughter, Elizabeth (died 1670) was the poet's last direct descendant.

We have no certain information as to Shakespeare's life between 1584 and 1592. There is an early tradition that he stole deer from Sir T. Lucy of Charlecote. We know Shakespeare was in London by 1592 but not when he went there. During these years Shakespeare must have acquired the varied knowledge and experience of life shown in his plays.

The mention of Shakespeare in a death-bed letter of the playwright Greene in September 1592, shows that as a writer for the stage Shakespeare was just becoming a serious rival to the university wits—Marlowe, Peele, Nashe, and Lodge. The years when the theatres were closed on account of plague gave time for the poems, *Venus and Adonis* (1593) and *Lucrece* (1594), both dedicated to the Earl of Southampton. By March 1595 Shakespeare was a shareholder in the acting company of the Lord Chamberlain's men who divided with the Admiral's men the command of the London stage from about 1594 to 1603. For this company, which later became the King's men, Shakespeare seems to have written during the rest of his career. After 1599 most of his plays were performed at the Globe Theatre. Shakespeare probably wrote his *Sonnets* between 1595 and 1600, but they were not printed till 1609.

In 1596 Shakespeare obtained a grant of arms; in 1597 he bought New Place, a substantial house and garden at Stratford, but he is still found living in London in 1597, 1599, and 1604. Shakespeare occasionally appeared as an actor himself, chiefly before 1598.

About 1610 Shakespeare retired to Stratford, and he wrote no more after 1613. He took no part in civic life, and died on April 23, 1616. There is no reason to reject the report that he died of fever contracted from drinking too hard at a merry meeting with Drayton and Ben Jonson.

TABLE OF APPROXIMATE DATES OF SHAKESPEARE'S PLAYS

1590–1.
2 Henry VI.
3 Henry VI.

1591–2.
1 Henry VI.

1592–3.
Richard III.
Comedy of Errors.

1593–4.
Titus Andronicus.
Taming of the Shrew.

1594–5.
Two Gentlemen of Verona.
Love's Labour's Lost.
Romeo and Juliet.

1595–6.
Richard II.
Midsummer-Night's Dream.

1596–7.
King John.
Merchant of Venice.

1597–8.
1 Henry IV.
2 Henry IV.

1598–9.
Much Ado About Nothing.
Henry V.

1599–1600.
Julius Caesar.
As You Like It.
Twelfth Night.

1600–1.
Hamlet.
Merry Wives of Windsor.

1601–2.
Troilus and Cressida.

1602–3.
All's Well That End's Well.

1603–4.

———

1604–5.
Measure for Measure.
Othello.

1605–6.
King Lear.
Macbeth.

1606–7.
Antony and Cleopatra.

1607–8.
Coriolanus.
Timon of Athens.

1608–9.
Pericles.

1609–10.
Cymbeline.

1610–11.
Winter's Tale.

1611–12.
Tempest.

1612–13.
Henry VIII.
Two Noble Kinsmen.

APPENDIX II

A NOTE ON SHAKESPEARE'S LANGUAGE

By C. T. ONIONS

VOCABULARY. As the *Oxford Shakespeare Glossary* shows, there are some ten thousand words in the whole of the works attributed to Shakespeare which require explanation for the general reader, either because they are no longer in ordinary use or because they are used by him in some way that is not now familiar. Among the former are such words as *ballow* cudgel, *fill-horse* shaft-horse, and *neaf* fist, which are now only provincial, and such others as *benison* blessing, *foison* abundance, *mow* grimace, *parlous* dangerous, *puissant* powerful, *teen* grief, which may be found still in literary diction, as well as a considerable number that have been used, so far as we know, by Shakespeare alone. With such as these we become acquainted by reference to glossaries and notes. But it is possible to continue to read Shakespeare without properly understanding him because we are unaware of, and sometimes do not even suspect, differences in the meaning of words that are in general use to-day. The following selection of such words will serve to indicate the nature of the differences that may be looked for.

allow approve
argument proof, subject of discourse
brave fine, splendid
churchman clergyman
close secret
complexion habit or constitution of body or mind, look, aspect, appearance
conceit idea, thought, invention
condition covenant, rank, character
difference disagreement, dispute
evil disease
fashion sort
favour appearance, face
feature bodily form
gear affair, business
grudge complain
hint opportunity
hope expect, suppose
infer allege
instance cause, evidence, proof
level aim
lewd bad, vile
liberal unrestrained, licentious
mere absolute, downright
merely entirely
miss do without
note sign, stigma, information
obsequious dutiful
owe own
painful laborious
passion painful disease, strong emotion
peevish silly, perverse
present immediate
presently at once
prevent anticipate
quality rank, profession
rate estimation
respect consideration
sad grave, serious
shrewd mischievous, bad
sort rank, class, way, manner
still always, continually
stomach inclination, angry or proud temper
sudden swift, violent
tall fine, valiant
type mark, badge
very true, complete

Among words having a very wide range of meaning the following may be noted:

humour (1) moisture, (2) any of the four fluids of the

human body recognized by the old physiologists, (3) temperament, (4) mood, temper, fancy, caprice, inclination;

nice (1) delicate, (2) shy, coy, (3) fastidious, (4) subtle, minute, (5) trivial, (6) critical, precarious, (7) exact, precise;

quaint (1) skilled, clever, (2) pretty, dainty, (3) handsome, elegant, (4) carefully elaborated;

sensible (1) sensitive, (2) of the senses, (3) capable of emotion, (4) rational, (5) tangible, substantial, (6) full of good sense;

wit (1) mental powers, mind, faculty of perception, as in *the five wits*, (2) inventive power, (3) understanding, intelligence, (4) wisdom, good sense, as in *brevity is the soul of wit*, (5) lively fancy producing brilliant talk.

A second adjective **dear** grievous, severe, dire (distinct from *dear* beloved, precious) is seen in *my dear offence*, *thy dear exile.*

Many adjectives and participial words show the application of a suffix with a force different from that which is now usual:

deceivable deceitful
tuneable tuneful
unmeritable undeserving
questionable inviting question
careless uncared for
cureless incurable
grac'd gracious
guiled treacherous
disdain'd disdainful
unexpressive inexpressible
plausive plausible
unavoided inevitable
beholding obliged, beholden
timeless untimely, premature

Note also the double meaning, active and passive, of **artificial** (1) constructive, creative, (2) produced by art.

Shakespeare uses a multitude of technical terms of the arts and sciences; these are treated in their historical setting in *Shakespeare's England* (O.U.P.); note especially the glossary of musical terms in vol. ii, pp. 32 ff. Some general aspects of the vocabulary are dealt with in G. S. Gordon's *Shakespeare's English*, Society for Pure English, Tract xxix (O.U.P.).

PRONUNCIATION. In order to understand the scansion of the verse it is necessary to bear in mind certain features of the pronunciation of the time. Many words of French or Latin origin had been variously stressed from early times, and deviation from present usage is to be seen, for example, in Shakespeare's *adver'tizèd, aspect', canon'izèd, chas'tise, compact'* (noun), *exile', instinct'* (noun), *obdu'rate, reven'ue, sepul'chre, solem'nizèd, triumph'ing*. The stressing of certain adjectives and participles of two syllables is subject to the rule that immediately before nouns of one syllable, and before other nouns stressed on the first syllable, they themselves are stressed on the first syllable, but in other positions on the second; thus: *all' the com'plete ar'mour, ev'ery way' complete'; the en'tire sum', your' entire' affec'tion; the crown' so foul' misplaced', the mis'placed John'*.

In words in *-ian, ience, -ient, -ion*, these endings may count as two syllables; thus, *Christian, patient* may be 3 syllables, *condition, impatience* 4, *lamentation* 5. Similarly *marriage* and *soldier* may be three syllables. There is variation in such words as *fire, hour, power, prayer*, which may count as either one or two syllables. *Either* may be slurred into one syllable, and *whether* is often so reduced, the form *where* frequently occurring in the old editions, continuing what was a regular early English variant form. *Hither, thither, whither*, and *having, evil, devil* are treated in the same way. *Statue* occurs in several passages in the old editions where three syllables are required; many modern editions substitute *statua*, which was a common Tudor and Stuart form.

NOUNS. The genitive singular ending *s* may be replaced by *his*, as *the count* his *galleys, Mars* his *armour*. The inflexion is dropped before *sake*, e.g. *for justice sake, for heaven sake*. Proper names often occur without inflexion, where the genitive might be expected, or *of*: e.g. *Venice gold, Rome gates, Tiber banks*. One of the adverbial uses of the genitive is preserved in *come your ways*. Notable examples of the *n*-plural are *shoon* for *shoes*, and *eyne* (eyes), which is used chiefly for rhyme. *Aches* is of two syllables, since the noun *ache* was pronounced *aitch*, as distinct from the verb, which was regularly spelt *ake* in the old editions. Names of measures and periods of time are often uninflected, as *twelve year, a thousand pound*: cf. *sennight* (= seven nights) week.

ADJECTIVES. Adjectives are converted into nouns with greater freedom than at present: *fair* is used for beauty as well as for lady, *the general* for the public, the multitude, *the subject* for the people of a state. Note the phrases: *in few* in few words, in short; *by small and small* little by little; *the most* (= majority) *of men*. *Enow* represents the old plural of *enough*, and is so used, always following its noun or pronoun. *Mo, moe* (= more) is also plural; it represents an old comparative adverb, which was used at first with a genitive, but became in time an adjective like *more*. The plural of *other* is either *others* or *other* (e.g. *and then come in the other*).

Peculiarities in the comparison of adjectives are: the use of the suffixes where we prefer *more* and *most*, as *certainer*, *perfecter*, *violentest*; the addition of *-er* to a comparative, as *worser*; the use of *more* and *most* with comparatives and superlatives, as *more better*, *most best*, *most dearest*, *more worthier*, *most worst*, *most unkindest*. Note the old comparative *near*, as in *ne'er the near*. An absolute superlative may be strengthened by prefixing *one*, e.g. *one the truest-mannered*.

PRONOUNS. The distinction between the familiar or contemptuous *thou* (*thee*, *thy*) and the respectful *ye* (*you*, *your*) is in general preserved. The old weak form *a* of *he* occurs in *There was a gaming*. The commonest genitive of *it* is *his*; the present-day *its* and the obsolete *it* (as in *It had* it *head bit off by* it *young*) are about equally frequent in the old editions. Pronominal possessive forms are sometimes used as adjectives, but only in company with other possessives, as in *his and* mine *lov'd darling*. Note the position of the possessive in *good* my *liege*, *sweet* my *coz*.

There is much irregularity in the use of the cases of pronouns. *Thee* is used for *thou*, as with intransitive imperatives, *look thee*, *stand thee close;* also in *I would not be thee*, and the like. We find also: *between you and I*; *Is she as tall as* me*?*; *Which, of* he *or Adrian . . . ?*; *Damn'd be* him . . . The functions of the original nominative *ye* and objective *you* are reversed in *I do beseech* ye, *if* you *bear me hard . . .*; *us* is usual for *we* in the interrogative *Shall*'s. There is no consistency in the use of *who* and *whom*; a common confusion is illustrated in whom *they say is killed*.

The relative pronouns are not discriminated according to present practice, since *which* may refer to persons and *who* to things. *The which* is very frequent; it may be used adjectivally, as in *For the which blessing I am at him upon my knees*. The nominative relative (the subject of the clause) is often absent, as in *There be some sports are painful.* After a negative or an interrogative, *but* is frequently used as a relative = that . . . not; e.g. *No man* **but** *prophesied revenge for it*; *What canst thou say* **but** *will perplex them more?*

VERBS. Verbs show many old forms as well as a variety of conjugation which are no longer possible in ordinary language.

Early strong forms are retained in *holp, holp'st,* alongside *helped, helped'st; spake* and *spoke* are both in use; old strong forms are replaced by weak in *becomed, shaked*; the past tenses *drunk* and *sprung* are more frequent than *drank* and *sprang*; the clipped *broke, spoke* occur beside the original participial forms *broken, spoken*; *catched* and *caught* are both found; many past tense forms are used for the past participle, as *eat, holp, forsook, rode, shook, swam.* Remarkable instances of the great variety of usage may be seen in *struck, strucken, stricken,* for the past participle of *strike,* and in the conjugation *write,* past tense *writ,* occasionally *wrote,* past participle *written, writ,* less frequently *wrote.* Weak verbs of which the stem ends in *d* or *t* often have shortened past participles, as *betid, heat, wed, wet.* Observe that *graft* and *hoist* are rather participles of the older verbs *graff* and *hoise* than of *graft* and *hoist.*

Present tense forms in *s* (including *is*) are not uncommonly used with plural subjects, especially where the verb precedes the subject; e.g. *What car***es** *these roarers for the name of king?*; *There* **is** *no more such masters.*

There are many survivals of impersonal uses, some of them in disguise. The older forms of *I were better, Thou'rt best* were *Me were better* It would be better for me, *Thee were best* It would be best for thee; but in *You were better* the case of the pronoun became ambiguous, *you* was in time felt as a nominative, and other pronouns fell into line. The history of the development of *I am woe* (in which *woe* is felt as an adjective) from the original *Me is woe* is somewhat similar. In *Fair befall thee* the verb is impersonal and *fair* an adverb.

The uses of the subjunctive are many and various. An exceptional construction is seen in **Live** *thou* (= if thou live), *I live.* An old use of the past subjunctive is exemplified in *If you would put me to verses, Kate, why, you* **undid** (= would undo) *me.*

The infinitive of a verb of motion is often to be supplied in thought with an auxiliary verb; e.g. *I* **must** *to England*; **Shall** *we to this gear?*

ADVERBS. Adverbs, especially those of one syllable, may have the same form as their corresponding adjectives, as *dear*, *full*, *fair*, *near*, *true*; such words as *excellent*, *equal*, *instant*, *prodigal* are also used adverbially. When two adverbs are coupled together which would both normally have the suffix *-ly*, one of them may lack it, as in *sprightful***ly** *and bold*, *so lame***ly** *and unfashionable*. A rare formation is *chirurgeonly* like a surgeon. Comparative forms with the suffix are used more freely than at present; e.g. *earth***lier** *happy*, *wise***lier**.

The use of *but* in the sense of 'only' needs to be specially noticed: *but now* just now, only this moment; similarly *but while-ere* only a short time ago, *but late* only lately. It is coupled redundantly with *only* in *He only lived but till he was a man*.

Normally, *only* should stand immediately before the words it modifies; but it is often loosely placed, as in *He only loves the world for him* (i.e. only for him).

A negative adverb (or conjunction) may be used with another negative word, superfluously from our point of view (the use was originally emphatic): *You know my father hath no child but I*, **nor none** *is like to have*. The negative may even be tripled: *Love no man in good earnest;* **nor no** *further in sport* **neither**. In the following a redundant negative occurs in a dependent clause after a verb of negative meaning: *You may deny that you were* **not** *the cause*.

PREPOSITIONS. Prepositions have many uses that differ from their present ones; for example, *for*, *of*, and *to* have each some ten meanings that are not current now. *Of* and *with* are both used to express the agent, as in *seen* **of** *us*, *torn to pieces* **with** *a bear*, or the instrument, as in *provided* **of** *a torch-bearer*, *killed* **with** *a thunderstroke*. With abstract nouns, *of* forms equivalents of the corresponding adjectives; e.g. *of desperation* desperate, *of nature* natural. Both *for* and *to* may be used, though in different kinds of context = in the character of, as: e.g. *turned out of all towns and cities* **for** *a dangerous thing*; *I have a king here* **to** *my flatterer*. A preposition is used freely at the end of the sentence or clause, e.g. *he I am before* = he in whose presence I am; sometimes it is redundant, as in *the scene wherein we play* in; or again, it may be dropped, as in *I see thou lovest me not with the full weight that I love thee* (i.e. *with*).

At in *at door*, *at gate*, and the like, is descended from the earlier *atte* (two syllables), which is for *at the*.

CONJUNCTIONS. The following should be noted: *an* or *an if* if; *as* as if; *for* because; *but* if . . . not, unless; *nor* . . . *nor* . . . neither . . . nor . . . , *or* . . . *or* . . . either . . . or . . .; *or ere* before ever; *so* provided that; *that* (in much wider use than at present) for the reason that, because, in order that, so that; *whiles* while.

The full exposition of the language of Shakespeare requires a book to itself, and such will be found in E. A. Abbott's *Shakespearian Grammar* and W. Franz's *Shakespeare-Grammatik*. An illuminating sketch is Henry Bradley's essay 'Shakespeare's English' in *Shakespeare's England*, vol. ii, pp. 539–74. Selected points are treated with some fullness in *Nine Plays of Shakespeare* (O.U.P.), pp. xix–xxxvi.

APPENDIX III

A NOTE ON METRE

SHAKESPEARE's plays are written in blank (i.e. unrhymed) verse with a varying proportion of prose and an occasional song in lyric metres in some plays. In *Richard II* there are only two lines of prose (v. v. 100–1), spoken by the unimportant Keeper of Richard's gaol. Almost one-fifth of the total number of lines in the play are in rhyming couplets, though here and there (e.g. II. i. 9–13) the poet slips into alternate rhymes or quatrains. The relatively high proportion of rhyme in the play is enough to mark it as one of fairly early composition. Rhyming couplets, either singly or in sequence, are used by the poet for a variety of purposes: (1) to mark the exit at the end of a scene (this occurs nearly everywhere throughout the play); (2) to mark exits during a scene, e.g. II. ii. 120–1; (3) occasionally, to mark an arrival, e.g. II. ii. 39–40; (4) for emphasis, e.g. I. i. 41–6, or (5) to mark the emphatic end of a longer speech, e.g. I. i. 150–1; (6) by splitting the couplet, to link the remarks of various speakers, e.g. I. i. 164–5, 174–5; (7) to create a kind of lyrical duet, as, for instance, in the scene of the parting of the King and Queen, V. i. 81–102. It is worth noting that Shakespeare seems to slip naturally into rhyme as the end of a scene approaches; for instance, at I. i. 196 ff., I. iii. 300 ff., II. i. 135 ff., &c., or wherever he wishes to give theatrical emphasis to what a speaker says, as at I. i. 175 ff., or I. iii. 85 ff. On the other hand where he seems himself to have been moved to genuine eloquence by the idea he is expressing, as in Gaunt's praise of England, or in Carlisle's and Richard's speeches in Act IV, rhyme is much less intrusive.

More than four-fifths of the lines of the play are in blank verse. This had been in use on the Elizabethan stage for a generation, and within the last ten years Marlowe had brought it to perfection in his 'mighty line'. Although all unrhymed verse might be called 'blank verse', the name is specially applied to the line consisting *normally* of ten syllables with five stresses or accents. It is common to use the terminology of classical verse and, if we understand that a long syllable in Latin or Greek corresponds to an accented or 'more conspicuous' syllable in English, we may describe blank verse as five iambic feet (i.e. five feet each consisting of an iambus, scanning ᴗ –). But whereas in classical verse quantity was rigid and the variations allowed from the pattern were strictly limited, in English verse very few lines conform absolutely to the pattern by having an equally strong accent on five of ten syllables. In Shakespeare not only is the accent either altogether absent, or reversed (– ᴗ for ᴗ –), in some feet, but often we have more, and occasionally fewer, than ten syllables in a line. A poet can make almost any departure from the norm, provided he does not destroy the sense of that pattern underlying his verse in the reader's mind. It is essential for all readers of Shakespeare first to acquire a consciousness of the pattern and for this purpose they may scan lines by stressing the syllables that should bear an accent, thus:

ᴗ – ᴗ – ᴗ – ᴗ – ᴗ –
The worst | is death | and death | will have | his day.
(III. ii. 103.)

The sense of this line in its context allows us to read it with some stress on all the syllables marked long and accented, but this is quite the exception. The other extreme is seen in the line 'Óld Jóhn | of Gáunt | tíme-hón | our'd Lán | castér' (I. i. 1), which must be pronounced as here marked, *not*, as the pattern would suggest, 'Old Jóhn | of Gáunt | time-hón | our'd Lán | castér'. Except for purposes of learning the pattern, we should always read by the sense and leave the metre to take care of itself. (For a brief treatment of Shakespeare's variations such as extra syllables, 'weak endings', &c., see Dowden's *Shakespeare Primer*, pp. 39, &c., and for a more general view of the subject E. Hamer's *The Metres of English Poetry*.)

APPENDIX IV

EXTRACTS FROM HOLINSHED

GLOUCESTER'S DEATH (cf. I. i. and ii)

RICHARD sent vnto Thomas Mowbraie, earle marshall and of Notingham, to make the duke secretlie awaie.

The earle prolonged time for the executing of the kings commandement, though the king would haue had it doone with all expedition, wherby the king conceiued no small displeasure and sware that it should cost the earle his life if he quickly obeied not his commandement. The earle thus, as it seemed, in maner inforced, called out the duke at midnight, as if he should haue taken ship to passe ouer into England, and there in the lodging called the princes In, he caused his seruants to cast featherbeds vpon him, and so smoother him to death; or otherwise to strangle him with towels (as some write). . . .

THE TRIAL BY COMBAT (cf. I. iii)

At the time appointed the king came to Couentrie, where the two dukes were readie, according to the order prescribed therein; comming thither in great arraie, accompanied with the lords and gentlemen of their linages. The king caused a sumptuous scaffold or theater, and roiall listes there to be erected and prepared. The sundaie before they should fight, after dinner, the duke of Hereford came to the king (being lodged about a quarter of a mile without a towne in a tower that belonged to sir William Bagot) to take his leaue of him. The morow after, being the day appointed for the combat, about the spring of the daie, came the duke of Norfolke to the court to take leave likewise of the king. The duke of Hereford armed him in his tent, that was set vp neere to the lists; and the duke of Norfolke put on his armor, betwixt the gate and the barrier of the towne, in a beautiful house, hauing a faire perclois of wood towards the gate, that none might see what was doone within the house.

The duke of Aumarle that day, being high constable of England, and the duke of Surrie, marshall, placed themselves betwixt them, well armed and appointed; and, when they saw their time, they first entered into the listes with a great companie of men apparelled in silke sendall, imbrodered with siluer, both richlie and curiouslie, euerie man hauing a tipped staffe to keepe the field in order. About the houre of prime, came to the barriers of the listes the duke of Hereford, mounted on a white courser, barded with greene & blew veluet imbrodered sumptuouslie with swans and antelops of goldsmiths woorke; armed at all points. The constable and marshall came to the barriers, demanding of him what he was. He answered: 'I am Henrie of Lancaster, duke of Hereford, which am come hither to doo mine indeuour against Thomas Mowbraie duke of Norfolke, as a traitor vntrue to God, the king, his realme, and me.' Then incontinentlie he sware vpon the holie euangelists, that his quarrell was true and iust, and vpon that point he required to enter the lists. Then he put vp his sword, which before he held naked in his hand, and, putting downe his visor, made a crosse on his horsse; and, with speare in hand, entered into the lists, and descended from his horsse, and set him downe in a chaire of green veluet, at the one end of the lists, and there reposed himselfe, abiding the comming of his aduersarie.

Soone after him, entered into the field with great triumph king Richard, accompanied with all the peeres of the realme, . . . The king had there aboue ten thousand men in armour, least some fraie or tumult might rise amongst his nobles, by quarelling or partaking. When the king was set in his seat, (which was richlie hanged and adorned,) a king at armes made open proclamation, prohibiting all men in the name of the king, and of the high constable and marshall, to enterprise or attempt to approch or touch any part of the lists vpon paine of death, except such as were appointed to order or marshall the field. The proclamation ended, an other herald cried: 'Behold here Henrie of Lancaster, duke of Hereford, appellant, which is entred into the lists roiall to do his deuoir against Thomas Mowbraie, duke of Norfolke, defendant; vpon paine to be found false and recreant!'

The duke of Norfolke houered on horssebacke at the entrie of the lists, his horsse being barded with crimoson velvuet, imbrodered richlie with lions of siluer and mulberie trees; and, when he had made his oth before the constable and marshall that his quarell was iust and true, he entred the field manfullie, saieng alowd: 'God aid him that hath the right!' and then he departed from his horsse, & sate him downe in his chaire, which was of crimson velvuet, courtined about with white and red damaske. The lord marshall viewed their speares, to see if they were of equall length, and deliuered the one speare vnto the duke of Hereford and sent the other vnto the duke of Norfolke by a knight. Then the herald proclamed that the trauerses & chaires of the champions should be remooued; commanding them on the kings behalfe to mount on horssebacke, and addresse themselues to the battell and combat.

The duke of Hereford was quicklie horssed, and closed his bauier, and cast his speare into the rest, and when the trumpet sounded set forward couragiouslie towards his enimie six or seuen pases. The duke of Norfolke was not fullie set forward, when the king cast downe his warder and the heralds cried, 'Ho, ho!' Then the king caused their speares to be taken from them, and commanded them to repaire againe to their chaires, where they remained for two long houres, while the king and his councell deliberatlie consulted what order was best to be had in so weightie a cause. Finallie, after they had deuised, and fullie determined what should be doone therein, the heralds cried silence; and sir Iohn Bushie, the kings secretarie, read the sentence and determination of the king and his councell, in a long roll, the effect whereof was, that Henrie duke of

Hereford should within fifteene daies depart out of the realme, and not to returne before the terme of ten years were expired, except by the king he should be repealed againe, and this vpon paine of death; and that Thomas Mowbraie, duke of Norfolke, bicause he had sowen sedition in the relme by his words, should likewise auoid the realme, and neuer to returne againe to England, nor approch the borders or confines thereof vpon paine of death; and that the king would staie the profits of his lands, till he had leuied thereof such summes of monie as the duke had taken vp of the kings treasuror for the wages of the garrison of Calis, which were still vnpaid.

When these iudgements were once read, the king called before him both the parties, and made them to sweare that the one should neuer come in place where the other was, willinglie; nor keep any company to gither in any forren region; which oth they both receiued humblie, and so went their waies. The duke of Norfolke departed sorrowfullie out of the relme into Almanie, and at the last came to Venice, where he for thought and melancholie deceassed: for he was in hope (as writers record) that he should haue beene borne out in the matter by the king, which when it fell out otherwise, it greeued him not a little. The duke of Hereford tooke his leaue of the king at Eltham, who there released foure yeares of his banishment: so he tooke his iornie ouer into Calis, and from thence went into France, where he remained. . . .

GAUNT'S DEATH AND RICHARD'S MISGOVERNMENT
(cf. II. i)

In this meane time [Feb. 3, 1399] the duke of Lancaster departed out of this life at the bishop of Elies place in Holborne. . . .

The death of this duke gaue occasion of increasing more hatred in the people of this realme toward the king, for he seized into his hands all the goods that belonged to him, and also receiued all the rents and reuenues of his lands which ought to haue descended vnto the duke of Hereford by lawfull inheritance; in reuoking his letters patents, which he had granted to him before, by vertue whereof he might make his atturneis generall to sue liuerie for him, of any maner of inheritances or possessions that might from thencefoorth fall vnto him; and that his homage might be respited, with making reasonable fine: whereby it was euident, that the king meant his vtter vndoing. . . .

This hard dealing was much disliked of all the nobilitie, and cried out against of the meaner sort; but namelie the duke of Yorke was therewith sore mooued; who, before this time, had borne things with so patient a mind as he could, though the same touched him verie neere, as the death of his brother the duke of Glocester, the banishment of his nephue the said duke of Hereford, and other mo iniuries in great number; which, for the slipperie youth of the king, he passed ouer for the time, and did forget as well as he might. . . .

THE CAPTURE OF RICHARD (cf. III. iii)

King Richard being thus come vnto the castell of Flint, on the mondaie, the eighteenth of August, and the duke of Hereford being still aduertised from houre to houre by posts, how the earle of Northumberland sped, the morow following being tuesdaie, and the nineteenth of August, he came thither, & mustered his armie before the kings presence; which vndoubtedlie made a passing faire shew, being verie well ordered by the lord Henrie Persie, that was appointed generall, or rather (as we maie call him) master of the campe, vnder the duke, of the whole armie. . . .

[Northumberland] came before the towne, and then sending an herald to the king, requested a safe conduct from the king, that he might come and talke with him; which the king granted, and so the earle of Northumberland, passing the water, entred the castell, and comming to the king, declared to him, that, if it might please his grace to vndertake, that there should be a parlement assembled, in the which iustice might be had against such as were enimies to the common-wealth, and had procured the destruction of the duke of Glocester, and other noblemen, and herewith pardon the duke of Hereford of all things wherein he had offended him, the duke would be readie to come to him *on his knees*, to craue of him forgiueness, and, as an humble subiect, to obeie him in all dutifull seruices. . . .

Then the earle of Northumberland, passing foorth of the castell to the duke, talked with him a while in sight of the king, being againe got vp to the walles, to take better view of the armie, being now aduanced within two bowe shootes of the castell, to the small reiosing (ye may be sure) of the sorow-full king. The earle of Northumberland, returning to the castell, appointed the king to be set to dinner (for he was fasting till then) and, after he had dined, the duke came downe to the castell himselfe, and entred the same all armed, his bassenet onelie excepted; and being within the first gate, he staied there, till the king came foorth of the inner part of the castell vnto him.

The king, accompanied with the bishop of Carleill, the earle of Salisburie, and sir Stephan Scroope, knight, (who bare the sword before him,) and a few other, came foorth into the vtter ward, and sate downe in a place prepared for him. Foorthwith as the duke got sight of the king, he shewed a reuerend dutie as became him, in bowing his knee, and, comming forward, did so likewise the second and third time, till the king tooke him by the hand, and lift him vp, saieng: 'Deere cousine, ye are welcome.' The duke, humblie thanking him, said: 'My souereigne lord and king, the cause of my comming at this present, is (your honor saued) to haue againe restitution of my person, my lands and heritage, through your fauourable licence.' The king hervnto answered: 'Deere cousine, I am readie to accomplish your will, so that ye may inioy all that is yours, without exception.'

Meeting thus togither, they came foorth of the castell, and the king there called for wine, and after they had dronke, they mounted on horssebacke, and rode . . . to London. . . .

THE ABDICATION OF RICHARD (cf. IV. i)

On Wednesdaie following, request was made by the commons, that sith king Richard had resigned, and was lawfullie deposed from his roiall dignitie, he might haue iudgement decreed against him, so as the realme were not troubled by him, and that the causes of his deposing might be published through the realme for satisfieng of the people: which demand was granted. Wherevpon the bishop of Carleill, a man both learned, wise, and stout of stomach, boldlie shewed foorth his opinion concerning that demand; affirming that there was none amongst them woorthie or meet to giue iudgement vpon so noble a prince as king Richard was, whom they had taken for their souereigne and liege lord, by the space of two & twentie yeares and more: 'And I assure you' (said he) 'there is not so ranke a traitor, nor so errant a theef, nor yet so cruell a murtherer apprehended or deteined in prison for his offense, but he shall be brought before the iustice to heare his iudgement; and will ye proceed to the iudgement of an anointed king, hearing neither his answer nor excuse? I say, that the duke of Lancaster, *whom ye call king*, hath more trespassed to K. Richard & his realme, than king Richard hath doone either to him, or vs:' . . . As soone as the bishop had ended this tale, he was attached by the earle marshall, and committed to ward in the abbeie of saint Albons.

Upon the morrow after, being tuesdaie, and the last daie of September, all the lords spirituall and temporall, with the commons of the said parlement, assembled at Westminster, where, in the presence of them, the archbishop of Yorke, and the bishop of Hereford, according to the kings request, shewed vnto them the voluntarie renouncing of the king, with the fauour also which he bare to his cousine of Lancaster to haue him his successour. And moreouer shewed them the schedule or bill of renouncement, signed with king Richards owne hand; . . .

[Richard] with glad countenance . . . said openlie that he was readie to renounce and resigne all his kinglie maiestie in maner and forme as he before had promised. And although he had and might sufficientlie haue declared his renouncement by the reading of an other meane person; yet, for the more suertie of the matter, and for that the said resignation should haue his full force and strength, himselfe therefore read the scroll of resignation, in maner and forme as followeth. . . .

THE DEATH OF RICHARD (cf. v. iv and v)

One writer, which seemeth to haue great knowledge of king Richards dooings, saith, that king Henrie sitting on a daie at his table, sore sighing, said: 'Haue I no faithfull freend which will deliuer me of him, whose life will be my death, and whose death will be the preseruation of my life?' This saieng was much noted of them which were present, and especiallie of one called sir Piers of Exton. This knight incontinentlie departed from the court, with eight strong persons in his companie, and came to Pomfret, commanding the esquier, that was accustomed to sew and take the assaie before king Richard, to doo so no more, saieng: 'Let him eat now, for he shall not long eat.' King Richard sat downe to dinner, and was serued without courtesie or assaie; wherevpon, much maruelling at the sudden change, he demanded of the esquier whie he did not his dutie: 'Sir' (said he) 'I am otherwise commanded by sir Piers of Exton, which is newlie come from K. Henrie.' When king Richard heard that word, he tooke his keruing knife in his hand, and strake the esquier on the head, saieng: 'The diuell take Henrie of Lancaster and thee togither!' And with that word, sir Piers entred the chamber, well armed, with eight tall men likewise armed, eurie of them hauing a bill in his hand.

King Richard, perceiuing this, put the table from him, &, steping to the formost man, wrung the bill out of his hands, & so valiantlie defended himselfe, that he slue foure of those that thus came to assaile him. Sir Piers, being half dismaied herewith, lept into the chaire where king Richard was woont to sit, while the other foure persons fought with him, and chased him about the chamber. And in conclusion, as king Richard trauersed his ground, from one side of the chamber to an other, & comming by the chaire, where sir Piers stood, he was felled with a stroke of a pollax which sir Piers gaue him vpon the head, and therewith rid him out of life; without giuing him respit once to call to God for mercie of his passed offenses. It is said, that sir Piers of Exton, after he had thus slaine him, wept right bitterlie, as one striken with the pricke of a giltie conscience, for murthering him, whome he had so long time obeied as king. . . .